THE
MYSTIC
VISION

THE

MYSTIC

VISION

DAILY ENCOUNTERS
WITH THE DIVINE

Compiled by

ANDREW HARVEY
AND ANNE BARING

HarperSanFrancisco
A Division of HarperCollinsPublishers

Text © 1995 *Andrew Harvey and Anne Baring*

Originally published by Godsfield Press Ltd 1995

Designed by *The Bridgewater Book Company Ltd*

 A GODSFIELD PRESS BOOK

1

First U.S. Edition

ISBN 0-06-063584-3

95 96 97 98 99 GDP 10 9 8 7 6 5 4 3 2 1

Take Courage for the Human Race is Divine

PYTHAGORAS

CONTENTS

INTRODUCTION

The mystics come back to us from an encounter with life's most august secret, as Mary came running from the tomb; filled with amazing tidings which they can hardly tell. We, longing for some assurance, and seeing their radiant faces, urge them to pass on their revelation if they can...

EVELYN UNDERHILL, *Mysticism*

All mystics speak the same language for they come from the same country.

LOUIS-CLAUDE DE SAINT-MARTIN

The mystics tell us that life is Divine, that we, in this dimension, are in the eternal embrace of the Divine. They show us that our sole purpose in life is to open our heart to this Divine Presence, to know it and love it as the essence and ground of our own lives and as the life of every creature and every aspect of creation. They invite us to recognize its longing to be known in our own longing for relationship with what seems so far from us yet is closer to us than our breathing. Ruysbroeck expressed this with perfect clarity: -

'When love has carried us above all things . . . we receive in peace the Incomprehensible Light, enfolding us and penetrating us. What is this Light, if it be not a contemplation of the Infinite, and an intuition of Eternity? We behold that which we are, and we are that which we behold; because our being, without losing anything of its own personality, is united with the Divine Truth.'

Ramakrishna said that the sensitive mother cooks fish differently for each of her hungry children – plain and bland for one, rich and spicy for the other. In exactly the same way, the Mother of the Universe reveals various spiritual approaches to the Divine. Whether you follow the idea of a personal God or the impersonal Truth, Ramakrishna said, you will certainly realize the One Reality, provided that you experience passionate longing for it.

There are an infinite number of perspectives and each one of them is a path to God. Each individual is unique and follows a unique path. With the longing to discover it, the way unfolds in the rhythm of the life of each separate being. Forcing the pace can block the opening of the heart. Each one of us will know the flowering of consciousness as it returns to the Source or Ground of Being. As Ramakrishna said, some will receive their meal early in the morning, others at noon, still others not until evening. But none will go hungry. Without exception, all living beings will eventually know their own true nature to be the Great Light.

The Alchemists knew their work of transmuting the lead of ignorance and separation into the gold of union would best be done gently, patiently and with great delicacy. As the windows of the heart are opened, the light pours in, revealing what was previously shrouded in darkness. Insight, wisdom, compassion grow with the experience of communion with the Divine.

In this book, we have gathered together from many different cultures, past and present, the magical, quickening words which guide and help us on our own journey of transformation. They transmit the vision of those women and men who discovered within themselves the quintessential treasure of the Divine. In a time as dark as ours they inspire and ennoble us all, giving us the hope, courage and strength to follow them into the heart of life.

ANNE BARING AND ANDREW HARVEY

JANUARY

THE DIVINE GROUND OF BEING

IKE A CHILD separated at birth from its mother, we are separated from the Ground of Being. This separation is experienced by us as an exile, a state of disharmony and disunion. From it has come our present dualistic, fragmented consciousness, and the fears and anxieties which torment us. But the memory of fusion or union with the Ground of Life lives on in us as a longing for reunion, for the ecstasy of belonging once again to that greater other. The mystics and sages of all times and cultures have tried to reveal to us what they have discovered: that we are in the Ground like a fish in the sea, like a bird in the air, and have tried to help us dissolve the illusion of our separate existence so that we would experience ourselves here and now, in this dimension, as what we truly are - Divine Being.

January 1

BENEATH the rose the desert grows,
Beneath the desert grows the sea:
How fathom that clear profundity,
End of all shadows and their source,
Blazing on which are spun
The Pole Star and the Sun.

Unpublished Poems
LEWIS THOMPSON

January 2

There was something formless yet complete
That existed before heaven and earth;
Without sound, without substance,
Dependent on nothing, unchanging,
All pervading, unfailing.
One may think of it as the Mother of all things under heaven
Its true name we do not know.

Tao Teh King
LAO TZU

January 3

The tao that can be told
is not the eternal Tao.
The name that can be named
is not the eternal Name.

The unnamable is the eternally real.
Naming is the origin of all particular things.
Free from desire, you realize the mystery.
Caught in desire, you see only the manifestations.

Yet mystery and manifestations
arise from the the same source.
This source is called darkness.

Darkness within darkness.
The gateway to all understanding.

Tao Teh King
LAO TZU

January 4

The simple, absolute and immutable mysteries of divine Truth are hidden in the super-luminous darkness of that silence which revealeth in secret. For this darkness, though of deepest obscurity, is yet radiantly clear; and, though beyond touch and sight, it more than fills our unseeing minds with splendours of transcendent beauty . . . And we behold that darkness beyond being, concealed under all natural light.

On The Mystical Theology
DIONYSIUS THE AREOPAGITE

January 5

PROFOUND and tranquil, free from complexity,
Uncompounded luminous clarity,
Beyond the mind of conceptual ideas;
This is the depth of the mind of the Victorious Ones.
In this there is not a thing to be removed,
Nor anything that needs to be added.
It is merely the immaculate
Looking naturally at itself.

NYOSHUL KHEN RINPOCHE

January 6

I n all things is shown the Face of faces, veiled and in a riddle. Howbeit unveiled it is not seen, until, above all faces, a man enter into a certain secret and mystic silence, where there is no knowing or concept of a face. This mist, cloud, darkness or ignorance, into which he that seeketh thy Face entereth, when he goeth beyond all knowledge and concept, is the state below which Thy Face cannot be found, except veiled; but that very darkness revealeth Thy Face to be there beyond all veils. Hence I observe how needful it is for me to enter into the darkness and to admit the coincidence of opposites, beyond all grasp of reason, and there to seek the Truth, where Impossibility meeteth us.

The Vision of God
NICHOLAS OF CUSA

January 7

We can speak no more of
Father, Son and Holy Spirit or of
any creature, but only of one
Being, which is the very substance
of the Divine Persons. There we
all are before our creation . . .
There the Godhead is, in simple
essence, without activity; Eternal
Rest, Unconditioned Dark, the
Nameless Being, the Superessence
of all created things.

The Seven Degrees of Love
JAN VAN RUYSBROECK

January 8

No words can describe it
No example can point to it
Samsara does not make it worse
Nirvana does not make it better
It has never been born
It has never ceased
It has never been liberated
It has never been deluded
It has never existed
It has never been nonexistent
It has no limits at all
It does not fall into any kind of category.

DUDJOM RINPOCHE

January 9

Now I shall tell thee of the End of Wisdom. When a man knows this he goes beyond death. It is Brahman, beginningless, supreme: beyond what is and what is not.

He is invisible: he cannot be seen. He is far and he is near, he moves and he moves not, he is within all and he is outside all.

He is the Light of all lights which shines beyond all darkness.

It is vision, the end of vision, to be reached by vision, dwelling in the hearts of all.

Bhagavad Gita xiii, 27-28

January 10

There is a Dream dreaming us.

African Bushman

January 11

Yet also it is good to know God perfectly; that is to say, he cannot be conceived by the mind, but knowing Him is to love Him; loving Him to sing in Him; singing to rest in Him; and by inward rest to come to endless rest . . . He truly knows God perfectly that feels Him incomprehensible and unable to be known.

The Fire of Love
Richard Rolle

January 12

The ultimate meaning and purpose of life cannot be expressed, cannot properly be thought. It is present everywhere, in everything, yet it always escapes our grasp. It is the 'Ground' of all existence, that from which all things come, to which all things return, but which never appears. It is 'within' all things, 'above' all things, 'beyond' all things, but it cannot be identified with anything. Without it nothing could exist, without it nothing can be known, yet it is itself unknown. It is that by which everything is known, yet which itself remains unknown. It is 'unseen but seeing, unheard but hearing, unperceived but perceiving, unknown but knowing' . . . We speak of 'God', but this also is only a name for this inexpressible mystery.

Return to the Centre
BEDE GRIFFITHS

January 13

We are not separate from Being, we are in it . . .

Ennead V, i,3
PLOTINUS

January 14

THE GROUND OF GOD and the Ground of the soul are one and the same.

MEISTER ECKHART

January 15

THE RIVER and its waves are one surf:
    where is the difference between
    the river and its waves?
When the wave rises, it is the water;
    and when it falls,
    it is the same water again.
    Tell me, Sir, where is the distinction?
Because it has been named as wave,
    shall it no longer be considered as water?

KABIR

January 16

God and the Godhead are as different from each other as heaven and earth . . . God *becomes* where all creatures express him: there he becomes 'God' . . . When I am come into the core, the soil, the stream, and the source of the Godhead, no one asks me where I am coming from or where I have been. No one has missed me in the place where 'God' ceases to become.

MEISTER ECKHART

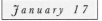

January 17

I think our concept of God is a product of our own dualistic thinking, which is that things are either transcendent or immanent. And I don't believe that anymore. Spirit and matter are not split in the manner that we have stereo-typically thought of it. My experience of God is of being transcendent and immanent all at once . . . I no longer believe that God is up there, and I don't believe that God is only within me, and I don't believe that God is merely out there in history. I think we are actually in God at all times.

SISTER MADONNA KOLBENSCHLAG

January 18

In this return in love in the divine ground every divine way and activity and all the attributes of the persons are swallowed up in the rich compass of the essential unity. All the divine means and all conditions, and all living images which are reflected in the mirror of truth, lapse in the onefold and ineffable waylessness beyond reason. Here there is nothing but eternal rest in the fruitive embrace of an outpouring love. This is the dark silence in which all lovers lose themselves.

The Adornment of the Spiritual Marriage
JAN VAN RUYSBROECK

T hus I learned that love is
our Lord's meaning. And
I saw full surely in this and in
everything else, that before God
made us, he loved us. And that
love was never ended nor ever
shall be. And in this love he has
performed all his actions; he has
made all things profitable to us.
And in this love our life is
everlasting. In our making we had
our beginning: but the love
wherein he made us is without
beginning . . . And all this shall
we see in God without end.

Revelations of Divine Love
JULIAN OF NORWICH

ALL THAT A MAN has here
externally in multiplicity is
intrinsically One. Here all blades
of grass, wood, and stone, all
things are One. This is the
deepest depth.

MEISTER ECKHART

January 21

He is beingness, both to himself and to all. And in that way only is he separated from all that is created, in that he is unconditioned being. And in that he is both one and all, all things are one in him and all things have their being in him, as he is the being of all.

THE BOOK OF PRIVY COUNSELLING

January 22

I am the one source of all: the evolution of all comes from me.

I am beginningless, unborn, the Lord of the worlds.
I am the soul which dwells in the heart of all things.

I am the beginning, the middle and the end of all that lives.
I am the seed of all things that are: and no being that moves or moves not can ever be without me.

KRISHNA
Bhagavad Gita

January 23

GOD speaking to Julian: I it am. The Might and Goodness of the Fatherhood; I it am; the Wisdom and Kindness of the Motherhood; I it am; the Light and Grace that is all blessed Love; I it am, the Trinity; I it am, the Unity: I am the sovereign Goodness of all manner of things: I am that maketh thee to love. I am that maketh thee to long. I it am, the endless fulfilling of all true desires.

Revelations of Divine Love
JULIAN OF NORWICH

January 24

I HAVE ONLY created man to adore me. I was a hidden treasure and wanted to be known. This is why I created the world.

The Koran

January 25

I am the Light that is above them all,
I am the All,
the All came forth from Me,
and the All attained to Me.
Cleave a piece of wood, I am there;
Lift up the stone, and you will find Me there.

The Gospel according to Thomas, logion 77

January 26

Listen, O beloved!
I am the reality of the world,
the center of the circle.
I am the parts and the whole.
I am the will holding Heaven and Earth in place.
And I have given you sight, only so you may see me.

IBN AL ARABI

January 27

IF IT IS SAID that I am concealed by the existence of the world, then who is it that blossoms in the form of the world? Can a red jewel be concealed by its own luster? Does a chip of gold lose its goldness if turned into an ornament? Does a lotus lose itself when it blossoms into so many petals? When a seed of grain is sown and grows into an ear of corn, is it destroyed or does it appear in its enhanced glory? So there is no need to draw the curtain of the world away in order to have my vision, because I am the whole panorama.

JNANESHWAR

January 28

I am the wind that breathes upon the sea,
I am the wave on the ocean,
I am the murmur of leaves rustling.
I am the rays of the sun,
I am the beam of the moon and stars,
I am the power of trees growing,
I am the bud breaking into blossom,
I am the movement of the salmon swimming,
I am the courage of the wild boar fighting,
I am the speed of the stag running,
I am the strength of the ox pulling the plough,
I am the size of the mighty oak,
And I am the thoughts of all people,
Who praise my beauty and grace.

The Black Book of Carmarthan

January 29

I am the supreme fiery force
That kindles every spark of life:
What I have breathed on will never die,
I order the cycle of things in being;
Hovering round it in sublime flight,
Wisdom lends it rhythmic beauty.

I am divine fiery life
Blazing over the full-ripened grain;
I gleam in the reflection of the waters,
I burn in the sun and moon and stars,
In the breeze I have secret life
Animating all things and lending them cohesion.

from a hymn of HILDEGARDE OF BINGEN

January 30

GLORY be to that God who is in the fire, who is in the waters, who is in the plants and trees, who is in all things in this vast creation. Unto that Spirit be glory and glory.

Svetasvatara Upanishad, Part 2

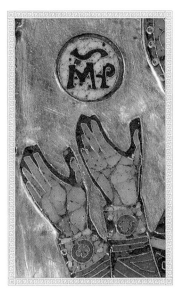

January 31

FLY AWAY, fly away bird to your native home,
You have leapt free of the cage
Your wings are flung back in the wind of God.
Leave behind the stagnant and marshy waters,
Hurry, hurry, hurry, O bird, to the source of life!

RUMI

FEBRUARY

ALL PATHS LEAD TO ME

Life is a challenge	· Meet it
Life is a gift	· Accept it
Life is an adventure	· Dare it
Life is a sorrow	· Overcome it
Life is a tragedy	· Face it
Life is a duty	· Perform it
Life is a game	· Play it
Life is a Mystery	· Unfold it
Life is a song	· Sing it
Life is an opportunity	· Take it
Life is a journey	· Complete it
Life is a promise	· Fulfil it
Life is a love	· Embrace it
Life is a beauty	· Praise it
Life is a spirit	· Realise it
Life is a struggle	· Fight it
Life is a puzzle	· Solve it
Life is a goal	· Achieve it

Seen in a draper's shop in India

February 1

Pilgrimage to the place of the wise is to find escape from the flame of separation.

RUMI

February 2

YOUR OWN Self-Realization is the greatest service you can render the world.

SRI RAMANA MAHARSHI

February 3

There are many ways to search but the object of the search is always the same. Don't you see that the roads to Mecca are all different? . . .The roads are different, the goal one . . . When people come there, all quarrels or differences or disputes that happened along the road are resolved . . . Those who shouted at each other along the road 'you are wrong' or 'you are an infidel' forget their differences when they come there because there, all hearts are in unison.

RUMI

February 4

The labyrinth is thoroughly known. We have only to follow the thread of the hero path, and where we had thought to find an abomination, we shall find a god. And where we had thought to slay another, we shall slay ourselves. Where we had thought to travel outward, we will come to the center of our own existence. And where we had thought to be alone, we will be with all the world.

The Power of Myth
JOSEPH CAMPBELL

February 5

LONG AND NARROW is the
ancient Path, – I have touched it,
I have found it – the path by
which the wise, knowers of the
Eternal, attaining to salvation,
depart hence to the high world
of Paradise.

Brhadaranyaka Upanishad

February 6

And in the ONE arose
love: Love the first seed
of the soul. The truth of this
the sages found in their
hearts: seeking in their hearts
with wisdom, the sages found
that bond of union between
Being and non-being.

Rig-Veda x

February 7

In any way that men love me in that same way they find my love: for many are the paths of men, but they all in the end come to me.

KRISHNA
Bhagavad Gita

February 8

Our work is the love of God. Our satisfaction lies in submission to the divine embrace.

JAN VAN RUYSBROECK

February 9

LET HIM WHO SEEKS, not cease seeking until he finds, and when he finds, he will be troubled, and when he has been troubled, he will marvel and he will reign over the All.

The Gospel according to Thomas, logion 2

February 10

Knock on yourself as upon a door and walk upon yourself as on a straight road. For if you walk on the road, It is impossible for you to go astray. And if you knock with Wisdom, You knock on hidden treasures . . . Wisdom is a holy kingdom and a shining robe.

The Teaching of Silvanus

February 11

THEREFORE, ANANDA, be ye lamps unto yourselves, be ye a refuge to yourselves. Betake yourselves to no external refuge. Hold fast to the Truth as a lamp; hold fast to the Truth as a refuge. Look not for a refuge in anyone beside yourselves.

THE BUDDHA

February 12

THE TAO is as deep as can be – who is willing to pursue it closely? If you don't go into the tiger's lair, how can you catch its cub? If you don't wash out the stone and sand, how can you pick out the gold?... carefully seek the heart of heaven and earth with firm determination. Suddenly you will see the original thing; everywhere you meet the source, all is a forest of jewels.

Awakening to the Tao
LIU I-MING

February 13

The nature of the one Reality must be known by one's own clear spiritual perception; it cannot be known through a learned man. Similarly, the form of the moon can only be known through one's own eyes. How can it be known through others?

The Crest-Jewel of Wisdom
SHANKARA

February 14

Believe nothing because a wise man said it,
Believe nothing because it is generally held.
Believe nothing because it is written.
Believe nothing because it is said to be divine.
Believe nothing because someone else believes it.
But believe only what you yourself judge to be true.

THE BUDDHA

February 15

RIGHTEOUSNESS, and sacred learning and teaching
Truth, and sacred learning and teaching
Meditation, and sacred learning and teaching
Self-control, and sacred learning and teaching
Peace, and sacred learning and teaching
Ritual, and sacred learning and teaching
Humanity, and sacred learning and teaching.

Taittirya Upanishad

February 16

D esolation is a file, and the endurance of darkness is preparation for great light.

Letter 1
ST. JOHN OF THE CROSS

February 17

H UMILITY is the Queen without whom none can checkmate the divine King.

The Interior Castle
ST. TERESA OF AVILA

February 18

A t that time, He will first open for them a tiny aperture of light, then another somewhat larger, and so on until He will throw open for them the supernal gates which face on all the four quarters of the world . . . For we know that when a man has been long shut up in darkness it is necessary, on bringing him into the light, first to make for him an opening as small as the eye of a needle, and then one a little larger, and so on gradually, until he can endure the full light . . . So, too, a sick man who is recovering cannot be given a full diet all at once, but only gradually.

The Zohar

February 19

But what is this transformation? The soul discovers its source of being in the Spirit, the mind is opened to this inner light, the will is energized by this inner power. The very substance of the soul is changed; it is made a 'partaker of the divine nature'. And this transformation affects not only the soul but also the body. The matter of the body – its actual particles – is transformed by the divine power and transfigured by the divine light – like the body of Christ at the resurrection.

Return to the Centre
BEDE GRIFFITHS

February 20

Up then, noble soul! Put on thy jumping shoes which are intellect and love, and overleap the worship of thy mental powers, overleap thine understanding and spring into the heart of God, into his hiddenness where thou art hidden from all creatures.

MEISTER ECKHART

February 21

Into deep darkness fall those who follow action. Into deeper darkness fall those who follow knowledge . . .

He who knows both knowledge and action, with action overcomes death and with knowledge reaches immortality.

Into deep darkness fall those who follow the immanent. Into deeper darkness fall those who follow the transcendent...

He who knows both the transcendent and the immanent, with the immanent overcomes death and with the transcendent reaches immortality.

Isa Upanishad

February 22

Through the mystery of this inner work darkness is turned into light. The chaos and confusion of our unconscious – what the alchemists termed the *prima materia* – gradually and miraculously reveal a higher centre of consciousness which is none other than our innermost essence, 'the face we had before we were born'. This is the Self, the Divine Child, which was always present within us, but hidden beneath layers of ego and conditioning.

LLEWELLYN VAUGHAN-LEE

February 23

Spiritual life is the bouquet,
the perfume, the flowering
and fulfilment of a human life,
not a supernatural virtue
imposed on it.

The Power of Myth
JOSEPH CAMPBELL

February 24

A MAN HAS many skins in
himself, covering the depths of his
heart. Man knows so many
things; he does not know himself.
Why, thirty or forty skins or
hides, just like an ox's or a bear's
so thick and hard, cover the soul.
Go into your own ground and
learn to know yourself there.

MEISTER ECKHART

February 25

Whoever knows the All but fails to know
himself lacks everything.

The Gospel according to Thomas, logion 67

February 26

I have just three things to teach:
simplicity, patience, compassion.
These three are your greatest treasures.
Simple in actions and in thoughts,
you return to the source of being.
Patient with both friends and enemies,
you accord with the way things are.
Compassionate toward yourself,
you reconcile all beings in the world.

Tao Teh King
LAO TZU

February 27

LET NOTHING disturb thee,
Nothing affright thee;
All things are passing;
God never changeth;
Patient endurance
Attaineth to all things;
Who God possesseth
In nothing is wanting,
Alone God sufficeth.

ST. TERESA OF AVILA
found on a bookmark in her Breviary

February 28

As a bee seeks nectar from all kinds of flowers
Seek teachings everywhere.
Like a deer that finds a quiet place to graze
Seek seclusion to digest
all that you have gathered.
Like a mad one beyond all limits
go where you please and live like a lion
completely free of all fear.

DZOGCHEN TANTRA

February 29

H e who sees that the Lord of all is ever the same in all that is, immortal in the field of mortality – he sees the truth.
And when a man sees that the God in himself is the same God in all that is, he hurts not himself by hurting others: then he goes indeed to the highest path.

Bhagavad Gita, xiii, 27-28

MARCH

THE FLUTE OF THE INFINITE: THE SPIRIT

Ramana Maharshi said, 'Silence is unceasing eloquence.' From the silence of the Presence, messages of love are trying to reach us at every moment from every corner of the universe. Always to be receptive to this music, and so learn how to live in compassionate harmony with it, is the goal of the realized life. As a Taoist master Chen Ting-Van wrote: 'The mind of the sage is empty and calm, profoundly calm, dealing with the world harmoniously, like bellows taking in air, like pipes containing music.' And in Proverbs 8:34 we read: 'Blessed is the man that *heareth* me, watching daily at my gates, waiting at the posts of my doors.'

March 1

he flute of the infinite is
played without ceasing
and its sound is love.

KABIR

March 2

There is a spirit in the soul,
untouched by time and flesh,
flowing from the Spirit, remaining
in the Spirit, itself wholly spiritual.
In this principle is God, ever
verdant, ever flowering in all the
joy and glory of His actual Self.

MEISTER ECKHART

March 3

By hearkening to the Name
man dives deep in an ocean of virtues;
by hearkening to the Name
the disciple becomes an apostle,
a prelate, a sovereign of souls.
By hearkening to the Name
the blind man sees the way;
by hearkening to the Name
Impassible streams are forded.

GURU NANAK

March 4

Holy Spirit
giving life to all life,
moving all creatures,
root of all things,
washing them clean,
wiping out their mistakes,
healing their wounds,
you are our true life,
luminous, wonderful,
awakening the heart
from its ancient sleep.

HILDEGARDE OF BINGEN

March 5

THE KING'S SON lies in the depths of the sea as though dead. But he lives and calls from the deep, 'Whosoever will free me from the waters and lead me to dry land, him will I prosper with everlasting riches.'

Splendor Solis
TRISMOSIN

March 6

Always dwelling within all beings is the Atman, the Purusha, the Self, a little flame in the heart. Let one with steadiness withdraw him from the body even as an inner stem is withdrawn from its sheath. Know this pure immortal light; know in truth this pure immortal light.

Katha Upanishad, Part 6

March 7

EACH MAN must discover this Centre in himself, this Ground of his being, this Law of his life. It is hidden in the depths of every soul, waiting to be discovered. It is the treasure hidden in a field, the pearl of great price. It is the one thing which is necessary, which can satisfy all our desires and answer all our needs . . . It is the original Paradise from which we have all come.

Return to the Centre
BEDE GRIFFITHS

March 8

he kingdom of heaven is like
unto a merchant man, seeking
goodly pearls: Who, when he had
found one pearl of great price,
went and sold all that he had,
and bought it.

Matthew 13: 45-46

March 9

 his is the precious pearl,
whose beauty is more
glorious, and whose virtue more
sovereign than the sun: It is a
never-failing comfort in all
afflictions, a balsam for all sores,
a panacea for all diseases, a sure
antidote against all poison, and
death itself; it is that joyful and
assured companion and guide,
which never forsakes a man, but
convoys him . . . into the blessed
paradise of perfect bliss.

Signaturum Rerum
JACOB BOEHME

March 10

The Tao is priceless, a pearl containing Creation. In storage, it is utterly dark, without a trace. Brought out, its light shines through day and night. Becoming wise depends entirely on this – you need nothing else to be enlightened.

Awakening to the Tao
LIU I-MING

March 11

The kingdom of heaven is like to a grain of mustard seed, which a man took, and sowed in his field:

Which indeed is the least of all seeds: but when it is grown, it is the greatest among herbs, and becometh a tree, so that the birds of the air come and lodge in the branches thereof.

Matthew 13: 31-32

March 12

WHO THEN are they that draw us and when shall come the Kingdom that is in heaven?

The fowls of the air and the beasts, whatever is beneath the earth or upon the earth, and the fishes of the sea, these they are that draw you. And the Kingdom of heaven is within you and whosoever knoweth himself shall find it. And having found it, ye shall know yourselves that ye are sons and heirs of the Father, the Almighty, and shall know yourselves that ye are in God and God in you.

Oxyrhynchus manuscript

March 13

CHRIST, supreme poet, lived truth so passionately that every gesture of his, at once pure Act and perfect symbol, embodied the transcendent. Baffling, like blinding light is this command of form.

Mirror to the Light
LEWIS THOMPSON

Abide in me, and I in you. As the branch cannot bear fruit of itself, except it abide in the vine, no more can ye except ye abide in Me.

❧

I AM the vine, ye are the branches. He that abideth in Me, and I in him, the same bringeth forth much fruit for without Me ye can do nothing.

John 15:4,5

I BELIEVE that God is in me as the sun is in the colour and fragrance of a flower – the Light in my darkness, the Voice in my silence.

HELEN KELLER

March 16

If I ascend up into heaven, thou art there:
If I make my bed in hell,
    behold, thou art there.
If I take the wings of the morning
    and dwell in the uttermost
        parts of the sea,
Even there shall thy hand lead me,
and thy right hand shall hold me.

Psalm 139

March 17

I am the light of the world,
He that followeth me shall not walk in darkness,
But shall have the light of life.

John 8:12

$$\boxed{March\ 18}$$

What cannot be spoken with words, but that whereby words
are spoken: Know that alone to be Brahman, the Spirit;
and not what people here adore.

⌒⌒

What cannot be thought with the mind, but that whereby the
mind can think: Know that alone to be Brahman, the Spirit;
and not what people here adore.

⌒⌒

What cannot be seen with the eye, but that whereby the eye
can see: Know that alone to be Brahman, the Spirit;
and not what people here adore.

⌒⌒

What cannot be heard with the ear, but that whereby the ear
can hear: Know that alone to be Brahman, the Spirit;
and not what people here adore.

⌒⌒

What cannot be indrawn with the breath, but that whereby
breath is indrawn: Know that alone to be Brahman, the Spirit;
and not what people here adore.

⌒⌒

Kena Upanishad, Part 1

March 19

WHOSOEVER drinketh of the water that I shall give him shall never thirst; but the water that I shall give him shall be in him a well of water, springing up into everlasting life.

John 4:14

March 20

Where all the subtle channels of the body meet, like spokes in the centre of a wheel, there he moves in the heart and transforms his own form into many. Upon OM, Atman, your Self, place your meditation. Glory unto you in your far-away journey beyond darkness!

Mundaka Upanishad

March 21

He comes to the thought of those who know Him beyond thought, not to those who imagine He can be attained by thought. He is unknown to the learned and known to the simple. He is seen in nature in the wonder of a flash of lightning. He comes to the soul in the wonder of a flash of vision.

Kena Upanishad

March 22

≈⌒≈

≈⌒≈

O HOW MAY I ever express that secret word?
O how can I say He is not like this,
    and He is like that?
If I say that He is within me,
    the universe is ashamed:
If I say that he is without me,
    it is falsehood.
He makes the inner and the outer
    worlds to be indivisibly one;
The conscious and the unconscious,
    both are His footstools.
He is neither manifest nor hidden,
    He is neither revealed nor un-revealed:
There are no words to tell that which He is.

KABIR

March 23

I am closer to you than yourself,
Than your soul, than your
own breath.
Why do you not see me?
Why do you not hear me?

IBN AL ARABI

March 24

I am thou and thou art I; and
wheresoever thou art I am
there, and I am sown in all; from
whencesoever thou willest thou
gatherest Me; and gathering Me
thou gatherest Thyself.

The Gospel of Eve

March 25

Fix thy mind on Me, give
thy heart's love to me,
consecrate all thy actions to My
service, hold thine own self as
nothing before me. To Me then
shalt thou come. Truly I promise
for thou art dear to Me.

Bhagavad Gita

March 26

Except a man be born again, he cannot see the kingdom of God.
· Except a man be born of water and of the Spirit,
he cannot enter the kingdom of God.
That which is born of the flesh is flesh;
and that which is born of the Spirit is spirit.
Marvel not that I say unto thee, Ye must be born again.
The wind bloweth where it listeth,
and thou hearest the sound thereof,
but canst not tell whence it cometh, and whither it goeth:
so is every one that is born of the Spirit.

John 3:3, 5-8

March 27

HE WHO IS near Me is near the
fire, and he who is far from Me is
far from the Kingdom.

*The Gospel according to
Thomas, logion 82*

March 28

This Self is the honey of all
beings, and all beings are the
honey of this Self.

Brhadaranyaka Upanishad

March 29

He that dwelleth in the
secret place of the most High
shall abide under the shadow
of the Almighty.

Psalm 91

March 30

I am a lamp to you who behold Me
I am a mirror to you who perceive Me
I am a door to you who knock at Me.
I am a way to you, a wayfarer.
You have Me for a couch; rest then upon Me.

The Acts of John

March 31

RADIANT IN HIS LIGHT, yet invisible in the secret place of the heart, the Spirit is the supreme abode wherein dwells all that moves and breathes and sees. Know him as all that is, and all that is not, the end of love — longing beyond understanding, the highest of all beings . . .

Mundaka Upanishad, Part 2, 2

APRIL

ADORATION, CONTEMPLATION, PRAYER

There is a worldwide famine of adoration and we are all visibly dying in it. The desolation, nihilism, meaningless, tragic and brutal carelessness and perversity we see all around us and in us is the direct result of living in a spiritual concentration camp in which we are starved, and have starved ourselves, of just that food our hearts, minds and souls need most – the food of worship, of love, of gratitude, of praise, the bread and the wine of adoration. We have forgotten how to renew ourselves in the fire and the light of the simple, divine glory of life itself and forgotten how to know that joy and light in us and around us that initiates and heals all who realize them and gives sacred fire to all true action.

Adoration is not some fervent spiritual or poetic exercise reserved for a chosen few. Adoration is nothing less than the oxygen of survival, the way itself to that illumination that alone can give us either the knowledge or the courage to save ourselves and nature now.

Adoration is both the way home and home itself, the sign and seal of true knowledge and the path to it, the radiant summit of the mountain of God and the force that gives the passion, the heart, the energy to scale it.

And the way of adoration is silence, contemplation, prayer.

April 1

O holy yoga of adoration, melting all fears
All places the false self could hide to save itself
To find the heart of the child behind the door of scars
That golden room where all things blaze.

ANDREW HARVEY

April 2

My sky and my earth cannot contain me
but I am contained entirely
in the heart of he who adores me.

Hadith

April 3

BEAUTY AND LOVE are as body and soul.
Beauty is the mine, Love is the diamond.

They have been together
since the beginning of time –
Side by side, step by step.

JAMI

April 4

All things of Thee partake
  Nothing can be so mean
  But with this tincture 'For Thy Sake'
  Shall not grow bright and clean.

A servant with this clause
  Makes drudgery divine;
  Who sweeps a room as for Thy laws
  Makes that and the action fine . . .

This is the famous stone
  That turneth all to gold,
  For that which God doth touch and own
  Can not for less be told.

GEORGE HERBERT

He held me to his chest
And taught me a sweet science.
Instantly I yielded all
I had – keeping nothing –
and promised then to be his bride.

I gave my soul to him
and all the things I owned were his:
I have no flock to tend
nor any other trade
and my one ministry is love.

If I am no longer seen
following sheep about the hills,
say that I am lost, that
wandering in love I let
myself be lost and then was won.

Poems
St. John of the Cross

April 6

I LIVE MY LIFE in growing orbits
which move out over the things of the world.
And I have been circling for a thousand years,
And I still don't know if I'm a falcon,
or a storm, or a great song.

Rainer Maria Rilke

April 7

Knowing is hard work, but loving is serene rest.

The Book of Privy Counselling

April 8

WHEN YOU are intoxicated with divine love, you see God in all beings.

The Gospel of Ramakrishna
SRI RAMAKRISHNA

April 9

I have dreamt of you
since the world began,
With a crown of peacock feathers on your head,
With robes of amber and yellow.
I see a garland of roses around your neck
As you take the cows out to graze.

MIRABAI

April 10

Deep in the wine vault of my love I drank, and when I came out on this open meadow I knew no thing at all . . .

Poems
ST. JOHN OF THE CROSS

April 11

The eye is not strong enough
  to look at the brilliant sun;
But you can watch its light
  reflected in water.
Pure Being is too bright to behold,
  yet it can be seen
  reflected in the mirror of this world.
For Non-Being
  is set opposite of Being,
  and catches its image in every moment.

MAHMOUD SHABISTARI

April 12

Each creature God made
  Must live in its own nature.
How could I resist my nature
  That lives for oneness with God?

The Flowing Light of The Godhead
MECHTHILD OF MAGDEBURG

April 13

Love is an infinite Sea whose skies are a bubble of foam.
Know that it is the waves of Love that turn the wheels of Heaven:
Without Love, nothing in the world would have life.
How is an inorganic thing transformed into a plant?
How are plants sacrificed to become rich with spirit?
How is spirit sacrificed to become Breath,
One scent of which is potent enough to make Mary pregnant?
Every single atom is drunk on this Perfection and runs towards It,
And what does this running secretly say but 'Glory be to God?'

RUMI

April 14

When the soul is plunged in the fire of divine love, like iron, it first loses its blackness, and then growing to white heat it becomes like unto the fire itself. And lastly, it grows liquid, and, losing its nature, is transmuted into an utterly different quality of being. And as the difference between iron that is cold and iron that is hot, so is the difference between soul and soul, between the tepid soul and the soul made incandescent by divine love.

de Quattuor Gradibus Violentae Charitatis
RICHARD OF ST. VICTOR

April 15

I experienced this state from evening prayer until one third of the night was over, and I heard the voices of the creatures in the praise of God, with elevated voices so that I feared for my mind. I heard the fishes who said, 'Praised be the King, the most holy, the Lord.'

DHU-L-NUN

April 16

When Barykh came to those
words in the psalm which read:
'I will not give sleep to mine eyes,
nor slumber to mine eyelids until
I find a place for the Lord,' he
stopped and said to himself:
'Until I find myself and make
myself a place to be ready
for the descending of the
Divine Presence.'

Tales of the Hasidim

April 17

Place your mind before the mirror of eternity!
Place your soul in the brilliance of glory!
Place your heart in the figure of the divine substance!
And transform your entire being into the image
of the Godhead Itself through contemplation.

ST. CLARE OF ASSISI

April 18

If you want to practice this Way, you must do it in the creative evolution of yin and yang of heaven and earth, realize its experience in the midst of all things and all events, and practice it and hold it in the presence of all people.

❧❧

This is work that is alive, effervescent, free, liberated, gloriously enlightened, true, and great. Do you think it can be attained by people who shut the door and sit quietly with blank minds?

Awakening to the Tao
LIU I-MING

April 19

True prayer and love are really learned in the hour when prayer becomes impossible and your heart turns to stone.

New Seeds of Contemplation
THOMAS MERTON

April 20

A s the flame clothes the black, sooty clod in a garment of fire, and releases the heat imprisoned therein, even so does prayer clothe a man in a garment of holiness, evoke the light and fire implanted within him by his Maker, illumine his whole being, and unify the Lower and the Higher Worlds.

THE ZOHAR

April 21

We will understand, when beginning to pray, that the bees are approaching and entering the beehive to make honey . . . When the soul does no more than give a sign that it wishes to be recollected, the senses obey it and become recollective. Even though they go out again afterward, their having already surrendered is a great thing.

The Way of Perfection
ST. TERESA OF AVILA

April 22

LET A MAN return into his own self, and there in the center of his soul, let him wait upon God, as one who listens to another speaking from a high tower, as though he had God in his heart, as though in the whole of creation there was only God and his soul.

ST. PETER OF ALCANTARA

April 23

 f all that God has shown me
I can speak just the smallest word,
Not more than a honey bee
Takes on his foot
From an overspilling jar.

MECHTHILD OF MAGDEBURG

April 24

THE WIDE pond expands like a mirror,
The heavenly light and cloud shadows play upon it.
How does such clarity occur?
It is because it contains the living stream
from the Fountain.

CHI HSI

April 25

Therefore we said: If to anyone the tumult of the flesh has fallen silent, if the images of earth, water, and air are quiescent, if the heavens themselves are shut out and the very soul itself is making no sound and is surpassing itself by no longer thinking about itself, if all dreams and visions in the imagination are excluded, if all language and everything transitory is silent . . . That is how it was when at that moment we extended our reach and in a flash of mental energy attained the eternal wisdom which abides beyond all things.

Confessions
ST. AUGUSTINE

April 26

I no longer try to change outer things. They are simply a reflection. I change my inner perception and the outer reveals the beauty so long obscured by my own attitude. I concentrate on my inner vision and find my outer view transformed. I find myself attuned to the grandeur of life and in unison with the perfect order of the universe.

Daily Word

April 27

SOLITUDE is resonant with a music as remote and vivid as the tremor of the stars. Out of all dream Athene arises grave, clear-eyed, forever youthful. About her a void tuned beyond all music, crossed by speedless intimations, threads of sound, of force, of light, more pure than frost.

Mirror to the Light
LEWIS THOMPSON

April 28

SILENCE LIKE SUNLIGHT will illuminate you in God, and will deliver you from the phantoms of ignorance. Silence will unite you with God Himself.

ISAAC OF NINEVEH

April 29

He is the real Sadhu, who can reveal
    the form of the Formless to the vision of these eyes:
Who teaches the simple way of attaining Him,
    that is other than rites or ceremonies:
Who does not make you close the doors,
    and hold the breath,
    and renounce the world:
Who makes you perceive the Supreme Spirit
    wherever the mind attaches itself:
Who teaches you to be still
    in the midst of all activities.

KABIR

April 30

By a green jade lake – what a wonderful sight:
    An old hermit fathoming Tao.
Aren't they the lucky ones – humble and still,
    Quietly humming the melodies of heaven?

The Book of the Heart
LOY CHING-YUEN

MAY

THE DIVINE MOTHER

IN JUDAISM, CHRISTIANITY AND ISLAM, the image of the ineffable mystery of life that we have called 'God' has contained no feminine dimension to balance its lonely masculinity. It has been defined solely in male imagery and has been conceived as transcendent to rather than immanent within life. Over the last two and a half thousand years, everything once associated with the Divine Feminine has been progressively excluded from Spirit: nature, matter, soul and body.

Yet now, the feminine image of the Divine is mysteriously permeating our consciousness. She is imagined, apprehended, experienced as the Divine Presence, the Divine Wisdom inherent in all forms of life, intrinsic to all levels of consciousness. Through vision, dream and intuitive perception she reveals the sacredness of life, the earth, matter, ourselves. She offers a new image of Spirit which embraces life in this dimension and unifies the spiritual and instinctual poles of our experience. She is transforming our image of reality.

The Divine Mother is close to us, not remote. She heals the separation between the divine and the human and brings to our consciousness a deeper vision, a new ethic of human responsibility towards the planet and the life it enfolds. She initiates a new phase in the evolution of human consciousness. Above all, she brings with her the sense of the beauty, balance and harmony of life. She asks us to discover, love and serve the Divine Life that she is.

May 1

May 2

One vision I see clear as life before me, that the ancient Mother has awakened once more, sitting on her throne rejuvenated, more glorious than ever. Proclaim Her to all the world with a voice of Peace and Benediction.

VIVEKENANDA

May 3

As truly as God is our Father, so truly is God our Mother . . . to the property of Motherhood belong nature, love, wisdom and knowledge and this is God.

Revelations of Divine Love
JULIAN OF NORWICH

The inhabitant or soul of the universe is never seen; its voice alone is heard . . . It has a gentle voice like a woman, a voice so fine and gentle that even children cannot become afraid. What it says is, 'Be not afraid of the universe.'

Alaskan saying

May 4

In the beginning, there was blackness.
Only the sea.
In the beginning there was no sun, no moon, no people.
In the beginning there were no animals, no plants.
Only the sea.

The sea was the Mother.
The Mother was not people, she was not anything.
Nothing at all.
She was when she was, darkly.

THE KOGIS

May 5

The first man knew her not
perfectly: no more shall the last
find her out. For her thoughts are
more than the sea, and her
counsels profounder than the
great deep.

Sir. 24: 28-29

May 6

Treasures of revelation
emerge from the Mother ocean . . .
Dive with abandon into her mystery.
You will discover a new gem every moment.

RAMPRASAD

May 7

THE VALLEY spirit never dies;
It is the woman, primal mother.
Her gateway is the root of heaven and earth.
It is like a veil barely seen.
Use it; it will never fail.

Tao Teh King
LAO TZU

May 8

My Mother is both within and without this phenomenal world . . . Giving birth to the world she lives within it. She is the Spider and the world is the Spider's web she has woven . . . The Spider brings the web out of herself and then lives in it.

The Gospel of Ramakrishna
SRI RAMAKRISHNA

May 9

PARADISE is at the feet of the Mothers.

Hadith

May 10

LIKE A MOTHER who protects her child, her only child, with her own life, one should cultivate a heart of unlimited love and compassion towards all living beings.

THE BUDDHA

May 11

I am the creation from the beginning
Everything in the creation is me.
All creation is growing toward me.
    It is begun in ecstasy
    It is continued in ecstasy
    It is sustained in ecstasy
    It will end in ecstasy.

Hidden Journey
ANDREW HARVEY

May 12

FROM THE SUMMIT of the
    world, I give birth to the sky!
The tempest is My breath, all
    living creatures are My life!
Beyond the wide earth, beyond
    the vast heaven,
My grandeur extends forever!

Rig Veda
DEVI SUKTA

May 13

I am the First and the Last . . .
I am the knowledge of my inquiry
And the finding of those who seek after me,
And the command of those who ask of me,
and the power of the powers in my knowedge
of the angels who have been sent at my word,
And of gods in their seasons by my counsel,
And of spirits of every man who exists with me,
And of women who dwell within me.

The Thunder, Perfect Mind

May 14

I WAS SET up from everlasting, from the beginning
or ever the earth was.
When there were no depths, I was brought forth,
When there were no fountains abounding with water.
Before the mountains were settled, was I brought forth . . .
When he prepared the heavens I was there:
When he set a compass upon the face of the depth:
When he established the clouds above:
When he strengthened the fountains of the deep:
When he gave to the sea his decree, that the waters
should not pass his commandment:
Then I was by him, as one brought up with him,
And I was daily his delight, rejoicing always before him . . .

Proverbs 23-25, 27-30

May 15

I am the Queen, source of thought, Knowledge itself. You do not know Me, yet you dwell in Me.

Rig Veda
DEVI SUKTA

May 16

I am the Invisible One within the All . . .
I am immeasurable, ineffable, yet whenever I wish,
I shall reveal myself of my own accord.
I am the head of the All.
I exist before the All, and I am the All,
Since I exist in everyone.

I am a Voice speaking softly.
I exist from the first.
I dwell within the Silence . . .
And it is the hidden Voice that dwells within me,
Within the incomprehensible, immeasurable Thought,
Within the immeasurable Silence.

Trimorphic Protennoia

May 17

I came out of the mouth of the most High,
   and covered the earth as a cloud.
I dwelt in high places,
   and my throne is in a cloudy pillar.
I alone encompassed the circuit of heaven,
   and walked in the bottom of the deep.
I had power over the waves of the sea, and over
   all the earth,
and over every people and nation.

Sir. 24: 3-6

I also came out as a brook from a river,
   and as a conduit into a garden.
I said, I will water my best garden,
   and I will water abundantly my garden bed;
and lo, my brook became a river,
   and my river became a sea.
I will yet make doctrine to shine as the morning,
   and will send forth her light afar off.
I will yet pour out doctrine as prophecy,
   and leave it to all ages for ever.
Behold that I have not laboured for myself only,
   but for all them that seek wisdom.

Sir. 24: 30-34

May 18

Listen with inward ear to the music
of her wisdom, teaching all creation.
With inward eye visualize her brilliant name,
Flowing across your heart in letters of molten gold.

RAMPRASAD

May 19

. . . AND THE SPIRIT of wisdom came to me . . . I loved her above health
and beauty, and chose to have her instead of light, for the light that cometh
from her never goeth out. And all such things as are either secret or
manifest, them I know. For wisdom, which is the worker of all things, taught
me . . . For she is the breath of the power of God, and a pure influence
flowing from the glory of the Almighty; a drop of dew that at the morning
cometh down upon the earth . . . For she is more beautiful than the sun,
and above all the order of stars: being compared with light, she is found
before it.

Wisd. 7:7,10,21,22,25,29

May 20

O Wisdom Goddess!
Your essence alone is present
    within every life, every event.
Your living power flows freely as this universe,
You are expressed fully, even by the smallest movement.
Wherever I go, and wherever I look,
I perceive only you, my blissful Mother,
radiating as pure cosmic play.
Earth, water, fire, air, space, and consciousness
    are simply your projected forms.
There is nothing else.

RAMPRASAD

May 21

Wishing to create an image of all beauty, and to manifest clearly to men and to angels the power of his art, God truly created Mary all-beautiful. In her He has brought together all the partial beauties which he distributed amongst other creatures, and has made her the ornament of all beings, visible and invisible; or rather, he has made her a blending of all perfections – divine, angelic, and human; a sublime beauty adorning two worlds, lifted up from earth to heaven, and even transcending that.

ST. GREGORY PALAMAS

May 22

HE CAME all so still
There his mother was,
As dew in April
That falleth on the grass.

❧

HE CAME all so still
To his Mother's bower
As dew in April
That falleth on the flower.

❧

HE CAME all so still
There his mother lay,
As dew in April
That falleth on the spray.

15th century carol

May 23

ail, height unattainable by human thought!
HAIL, depth invisible even to the eyes of angels!
Hail to you through whom creation is reborn!
Hail to you through whom the Creator becomes a child!
Hail, vine of the unwithered shoot!
Hail, field of the immortal crop!
Hail, to you who harvest the harvester, friend of man!
Hail to you who plant the planter of our life!
Hail, field that flourishes with a fertility of compassion!
Hail, table that bears a wealth of mercy!
Hail to you who make a meadow of delight to blossom!
Hail to you who make ready a haven for souls!
Hail, rock giving water to those who thirst for life!
Hail, pillar of fire, leading those in darkness!

May 24

Hail, branch of fair-shading leaves, under whom many take shelter!
Hail to you who bring opposites together!
Hail to you who have filled the nets of the fishermen!
Hail to you who draw forth from the depths of ignorance!
Hail, boat for those who wish to be saved!
Hail, harbour for the sailors of life!
Hail, inexhaustible treasure of life!

Akathist Hymn to Mary

May 25

Salutations to Her who keeps all the worlds under her sway
Salutations to Her who grants all our desires
Salutations to Her whose form is existence-knowledge-bliss
Salutations to Her who is not limited by space and time
Salutations to Her who is present in all as the inner controller
Salutations to Her who casts her spell on all.

From the Sri Lalita Sahasranama

May 26

She is the inmost awareness
of the sage who realizes
that Consciousness alone exists.
She is the life blossoming within
the creatures of the universe.
Both macrocosm and microcosm
are lost within Mother's Womb . . .

When anyone attempts to know Her,
the singer of this song laughs.
Can you swim across
a shoreless ocean?
Yet the child in me still
reaches out to touch the moon.

RAMPRASAD

May 27

LIKE A BEAUTIFUL white dove,
  That rises from the middle of the waters
And comes to shake its wings out over the earth,
  The Holy Spirit emanates from the Infinite ocean
of the Divine perfections and comes
  to beat Her wings out over clear souls
To distill in them the balm of love.

CURÉ D'ARS

May 28

The Presence he yearned for suddenly drew close.
  Across the silence of the Ultimate Calm,
  Out of a marvellous Transcendence came
  A body of wonder and translucency
  As if a sweet mystic summary of her Self
  Escaping into the original Bliss
  Had come enlarged out of eternity,
  Someone came infinite and absolute.
  A being of wisdom, power and delight,
  Even as a mother draws her child into her arms,
  Took to her breast nature and world and soul.

Savitri, Book 8
SRI AUROBINDO

May 29

WHO CAN EVER know God? I don't even try. I only call on Him as Mother. Let Mother do whatever She likes. I shall know Her if it is Her will: but I shall be happy to remain ignorant if She wills otherwise . . . The young child wants only his mother. He doesn't know how wealthy his mother is, and he doesn't even want to know. He knows only 'I have a mother, why should I worry?'

The Gospel of Ramakrishna
SRI RAMAKRISHNA

May 30

O my Mother Nut,
Stretch your wings over me;
Let me become like the imperishable stars,
like the indefatigable stars.
O Great Being who is in the world of the dead
At whose feet is Eternity,
In whose hand is the Always,
Come to me.
O great divine beloved Soul,
Who is in the mysterious abyss
Come to me.

Egyptian inscription

May 31

O Greening Branch
You stand in your nobility
Like the rising dawn.
Rejoice now and exult
And deign to free the fools we are
From our long slavery to evil
And hold out your hand
To raise us up.

HILDEGARDE OF BINGEN

JUNE

WORDLESS MYSTERIES:
THE MYSTIC VISION

The real war in the modern world is not between democracy and communism or between capitalism and totalitarianism or between liberalism and fascism. It is the war for the mind and heart of humankind between two completely different versions of reality: the version that materialist science, most contemporary philosophy and most modern art gives human beings, as driven, dying animals in a random universe (a version that many institutionalized religions unconsciously abet with their emphasis on human sinfulness and powerlessness) and that version of humankind's essential divine destiny that mystics in all ages have discovered and struggled to keep alive. This latter version can be summed up in the wonderful words of the great Sufi master Al Ghazzali: 'Know, O Beloved, Man was not created in jest or at random, but marvelously made for some great end,' or in the words of Pythagoras: 'Take courage, for the human race is divine,' or in the call to transcendence of the central Hindu scripture, the Bhagavad Gita: 'He is forever free who has broken out of the ego cage of I and mine to be united with the lord of Love.'

June 1

God wants the heart.

TALMUD

June 2

Every particle of the world is a mirror,
In each atom lies the blazing light
    of a thousand suns.
Cleave the heart of a rain-drop,
    a hundred pure oceans will flow forth.
Look closely at a grain of sand,
    the seed of a thousand beings can be seen . . .
Within the pulp of a millet seed
    an entire universe can be found.
In the wing of a fly,
    an ocean of wonder;
In the pupil of the eye, an endless heaven.
Though the inner chamber of the heart is small,
    the Lord of both worlds
    gladly makes His home there.

MAHMUD SHABISTARI

June 3

Inside ourselves or nowhere is eternity with its worlds, the past and the future . . . Now, 'inside' appears to us so dark, lonely, shapeless, but how differently will it appear once this darkening has passed.

NOVALIS

June 4

No matter how deeply I go into myself my God is dark, and like a webbing made of a hundred roots, that drink in silence.

RAINER MARIA RILKE

June 5

THE DIVINE DARK is the inaccessible Light in which God is said to dwell. Into this dark, invisible because of its surpassing brightness and unsearchable because of the abundance of its supernatural torrents of light, all enter who are deemed worthy to know and see God: and, by the very fact of not seeing or knowing, are truly *in* Him who is above all sight and knowledge.

Letter to Dorothy the Deacon
DIONYSIUS THE AREOPAGITE

June 6

THE IMAGE of God is found essentially and personally in all mankind. Each possesses it whole, entire and undivided, and all together not more than one alone. In this way we are all one, intimately united in our eternal image, which is the image of God and the source in us of all our life.

The Adornment of the Spiritual Marriage
JAN VAN RUYSBROECK

June 7

Hear from the heart wordless mysteries!
Understand what cannot be understood!
In man's stone-dark heart there burns a fire
That burns all veils to their root and foundation.
When the veils are burned away, the heart will understand completely . . .
Ancient Love will unfold ever-fresh forms
In the heart of the Spirit, in the core of the heart.

RUMI

June 8

The entire effort of our Soul is to become God. This effort is as natural to man as that of flying is to birds. For it is inherent in all men, everywhere and always: therefore it does not follow the incidental quality of some man, but the nature of the species itself . . . For who implanted in our Souls this (tendency toward God) but God Himself, whom we seek?

MARSILIO FICINO

June 9

here is a mode of knowing that is above intelligence, a divine madness. The like alone knows the like; sense, the sensible; intelligence, intelligence; the one, that which is one. Let but the intelligent soul transcend intelligence, and it forgets itself and the rest. Adhering to unity, it therein peacefully dwells, closed to all knowledge, mute and silent . . . this, my friend, is the divine working of the soul: he who is capable of it is set free from the bonds of authority; he is sheltered, not only from exterior but also from interior impulses: he is made God.

PROCLUS

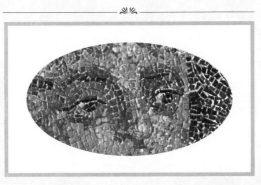

June 10

Imagination is the star in man, the celestial or super-celestial body.

RULAND THE LEXICOGRAPHER

June 11

I cease not from my great task
To open the Eternal Worlds, to open the
Immortal Eye
Of man inwards into the Realms of Thought,
into Eternity
Ever expanding in the Bosom of God, the
Human Imagination.

WILLIAM BLAKE

June 12

The essence of the First Absolute Light, God, gives constant illumination, whereby it is manifested and it brings all things into existence, giving life to them by its rays. Everything in the world is derived from the Light of His Essence; all beauty and perfection are the gift of His Bounty; and to attain fully to this illumination is salvation.

The Empurpled Angel
SOHRAWARDI

June 13

Radiant in his light, yet invisible in the secret place of the heart, the Spirit is the supreme abode wherein dwells all that moves and breathes and sees.

Our whole business, therefore, in this life is to restore to health the eye of the heart whereby God may be seen.

ST. AUGUSTINE

June 14

The eye with which I see God is the same as that with which he sees me. My eye and the eye of God are one eye, one vision, one knowledge, and one love.

MEISTER ECKHART

June 15

I am blind and do not see the things of this world; but when the light comes from Above, it enlightens my Heart and I can see, for the Eye of my Heart sees everything: and through this vision I can help my people. The heart is a sanctuary at the Center of which there is a little space, wherein the Great Spirit dwells, and this is the Eye. This is the Eye of *Wakantanka* by which He sees all things, and through which we see Him.

BLACK ELK

June 16

You will never enjoy the world aright till the sea itself floweth in your veins, till you are clothed with the heavens and crowned with the stars; and perceive yourself to be the sole heir of the whole world, and more than so, because men are in it who are every one the whole heirs as well as you. Till you can sing and rejoice and delight in God, as misers do in gold, and Kings in sceptres, you never enjoy the world.

Centuries of Meditations
THOMAS TRAHERNE

June 17

The ever-new magical universe
is continually reborn in the child.
Only the grown up was banished
from Eden. The child eats of the
tree of life. For him the laws of
the universe are magical. This
childhood and this magic the
Christ restores.

Mirror to the Light
LEWIS THOMPSON

June 18

KNOW, O my son, that each
thing in the universe is a vessel
full to the brim with wisdom and
beauty. It is a drop from the river
of His Beauty . . . It is a hidden
treasure because of its fullness. It
has exploded and made the earth
more brilliant than the skies. It has
sprung up and made the earth like
a sultan wearing a robe of satin.

RUMI

June 19

In all the ten directions of the universe,
There is only one truth.
When we see clearly, the great teachings are the same.

RYOKAN

June 20

Generation upon generation has passed, my friend, but these meanings are constant and everlasting. The water in the stream may have changed many times, but the reflection of the moon and the stars remains the same.

RUMI

June 21

There is a Spirit who is hidden in all things, as cream is hidden in milk, and who is the source of self-knowledge and self-sacrifice. This is Brahman, the Spirit Supreme.

Svetasvatara Upanishad, Part 1

June 22

In the deeper reality beyond space and time, we may be all members of one body.

SIR JAMES JEANS

June 23

GOD HAS created us in order that we may become partakers of the divine nature, in order that we might enter into eternity, and that we might appear like unto Him, being deified by that grace out of which all things that exist have come.

ST. MAXIMUS THE CONFESSOR

June 24

God does not proclaim Himself. He is everybody's secret.

Katha Upanishad

June 25

The best treasure that a man can attain unto in this world is true knowledge; *even the knowledge of himself.* For *man* is the great mystery of God, the microcosm, or complete abridgement of the whole universe: he is the *mirandum Dei opus*, God's masterpiece, a living emblem and hieroglyphic of eternity and time; and therefore to know whence he is, and what his temporal and eternal being and well-being are, must needs be that *one* necessary thing, to which all our chief study should aim, and in comparison of which all the wealth of this world is but dross, and a loss to us.

Signaturum Rerum
JACOB BOEHME

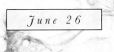

June 26

Fish cannot drown in water
Birds cannot sink in air.
Gold cannot perish in the refiner's fire.
This has God given to all creatures,
To foster and seek their own nature.
How then can I withstand mine?

The Flowing Light of the Godhead
MECHTHILD OF MAGDEBURG

June 27

How great is the difference
between the secret friend and the
hidden child! For the friend makes
only loving, living but measured
ascents towards God. But the child
presses on to lose his own life upon
the summits, in that simplicity
which knoweth not itself.

The Sparkling Stone
JAN VAN RUYSBROECK

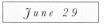

June 28

When we transcend ourselves and become in our ascent towards God so simple that the bare supreme Love can lay hold of us, then we cease, and we and all our selfhood die in God. And in this death we become the hidden children of God, and find a new life within us.

The Sparkling Stone
JAN VAN RUYSBROECK

June 29

An effortless compassion can arise for all beings who have not realized their true nature. So limitless is it that if tears could express it, you would cry without end. You are naturally liberated from all suffering and fear. Then if you were to speak of the joy and bliss that arise from this realization, it is said by the Buddhas that if you were to gather all the glory, enjoyment, pleasure and happiness of the world and put it together, it would not approach one tiny fraction of the bliss that you experience upon realizing the nature of mind.

NYOSHUL KENPO

June 30

Everything you see has its roots in the unseen world.
The forms may change, yet the essence remains the same.
Every wonderful sight will vanish, every sweet word will fade,
But do not be disheartened,
The source they come from is eternal, growing,
Branching out, giving new life and new joy.
Why do you weep?
The source is within you
And this whole world is springing up from it.

RUMI

JULY

THE GLORY OF CREATION

When the eyes of the heart are opened, the creation is revealed as it really is, the body of the Divine Light. Everything in it is shown irradiated naturally by Light and known as utterly sacred and holy. Being initiated into this glory is essential for all of us now for it is only by knowing what nature really is and in what a splendid divine theatre we are that we will find in ourselves the hope and energy and passion necessary to do everything in our power to protect the planet and all the miraculous life it enfolds.

We can discover how to attune ourselves to the music of this one Life. We can nurture in ourselves the vision of the child, the poet, the artist, and those who live close to nature. We can learn how to heal the heart. Healing the heart is about cherishing in every sense: cherishing the soul which has been neglected for so many centuries; cherishing the body which has been despised and rejected; cherishing the lives which have been entrusted to us; cherishing the Earth which is the great field of all our endeavours.

July 1

The world is charged with the grandeur of God.
　It will flame out, like shining from shook foil;
　It gathers to a greatness, like the ooze of oil
Crushed. Why do men then now not reck his rod?
Generations have trod, have trod, have trod;
　　And all is seared with trade; bleared, smeared with toil;
　　And wears man's smudge and shares man's smell: the soil
Is bare now, nor can foot feel, being shod.

And for all this, nature is never spent;
　There lives the dearest freshness deep down things;
And though the last lights off the black West went
　Oh, Morning, at the brown brink eastward, springs –
Because the Holy Ghost over the bent
　World broods with warm breast and with ah! bright wings.

GERARD MANLEY HOPKINS

July 2

THE WORLD is a mirror of infinite beauty, yet no man sees it. It is a Temple of majesty, yet no man regards it. It is a region of Light and Peace, did not men disquiet it. It is the Paradise of God. It is more to man since he is fallen than it was before. It is the place of Angels and the Gate of Heaven.

Centuries of Meditations
THOMAS TRAHERNE

July 3

The Kingdom of the Father is spread upon the earth and men do not see it.

The Gospel according to Thomas, logion 113

July 4

For everything that lives is holy.

WILLIAM BLAKE

July 5

Hidden Nature is secret God.

The Life Divine
SRI AUROBINDO

July 6

Each bush and oak doth know
I AM.

HENRY VAUGHAN

July 7

There is one common flow,
one common breathing, all
things are in sympathy.

HIPPOCRATES

July 8

It was suddenly revealed to me that everything is pure spirit. The utensils of worship, the altar, the door frames, all pure spirit. Men, animals and other beings – all pure spirit. Then, like a madman, I began to shower flowers in all directions. Whatever I saw, I worshipped.

The Gospel of Ramakrishna
SRI RAMAKRISHNA

July 9

IF WE HAVE a wonderful sense of the divine, it is because we live amid such awesome magnificence. If we have refinement of emotion and sensitivity, it is because of the delicacy, the fragrance, the indescribable beauty of song and music and rhythmic movement in the world about us.

The Dream of the Earth
THOMAS BERRY

July 10

Never was anything in the world loved too much, but many things have been loved in a false way; and all in too short a measure.

Centuries of Meditations

July 11

We are the miracles that God made
To taste the bitter fruit of Time.
We are precious.
And one day our suffering
Will turn into the wonders of the earth . . .

❧

That is why our music is so sweet.
It makes the air remember.
There are secret miracles at work
That only Time will bring forth.
I too have heard the dead singing.

❧

And they tell me that
This life is good
They tell me to live it gently
With fire, and always with hope.
There is wonder here

❧

And there is surprise
In everything the unseen moves.
The ocean is full of songs.
The sky is not an enemy.
Destiny is our friend.

An African Elegy
BEN OKRI

July 12

Holy Mother Earth, the
trees and all nature, are witnesses
to your thoughts and deeds.

A Winnebago wise saying

July 13

I f you will think of ourselves
as coming out of the
earth, rather than having been
thrown in here from somewhere
else, you see that we are the
earth, we are the consciousness of
the earth. These are the eyes of
the earth. And this is the voice of
the earth.

The Power of Myth
JOSEPH CAMPBELL

July 14

The Earth, its life am I,
The Earth, its feet are my feet,
The Earth, its legs are my legs,
The Earth, its body is my body,
The Earth, its thoughts are my thoughts,
The Earth, its speech is my speech.

Navajo Chant

July 15

We always make offerings to the sun
 And to the mountains
And to the stars.
 That is why we live here . . .
We are the Elder Brothers.
 We have not forgotten the old ways.
How could I say that I do not know how to dance?
 We still know how to dance.
We have forgotten nothing.
 We know how to call the rain.
If it rains too hard we know how to stop it.
 We call the summer.
We know how to bless the world and make it flourish.

THE KOGIS

July 16

Do NOT go into the garden of flowers!
 O Friend! go not there;
In your body is the garden of flowers.
Take your seat on the thousand petals
 of the lotus, and there gaze on the
 Infinite Beauty.

KABIR

July 17

HERE in this body are the sacred
rivers: here are the sun and moon,
as well as the pilgrimage places.
I have not encountered another
temple as blissful as my own body.

SARAHA

July 18

Do not disdain your body
For the soul is just as safe in its
body as in the Kingdom of Heaven.

MECHTHILD OF MAGDEBURG

July 19

The body also has an
experience of divine things,
when the passionate forces of the
soul are not put to death but
transformed and sanctified.

ST. GREGORY PALAMAS

July 20

With beauty before me, I walk
With beauty behind me, I walk
With beauty above me, I walk
With beauty below me, I walk
From the East, beauty has been restored
From the South, beauty has been restored
From the West, beauty has been restored
From the North, beauty has been restored
From the zenith in the sky beauty has been restored
From the nadir of the earth beauty has been restored
From all around me beauty has been restored.

Navajo prayer

July 21

Every vision born of earth is fleeting
Every vision born of heaven is a blessing
For people, the sight of spring warms their hearts
For fish, the rhythm of the ocean is a blessing
The brilliant sun that shines in every heart
For the heaven's earth and all creatures
What a blessing! . . .
The heart can't wait to speak of this ecstasy
The soul is kissing the earth, saying
Oh God, what a blessing!

RUMI

July 22

Oh the lark in the morning
She rises from her nest
And she comes here in the
evening with the jewel in
her breast.

JOHN CLARE

July 23

There was a time when
meadow, grove,
And stream,
The earth, and every
common sight,
To me did seem
Apparelled in celestial light,
The glory and the freshness
of a dream.

WILLIAM WORDSWORTH

July 24

R amakrishna said, 'The Gopis see Krishna in everything: to them the whole world is filled with Krishna. They said that they themselves were Krishna. Looking at the trees, they said, "These are hermits absorbed in meditation on Krishna." Looking at the grass, they said, "The hair of the earth is standing on end at the touch of Krishna." '

The Gospel of Ramakrishna

July 25

I listen and hear the Silence
I listen and see the Silence
I listen and taste the Silence
I listen and smell the Silence
I listen and embrace the Silence

TWYLAH NITSCH

July 26

Over our striving, our rooms, our houses; the beautiful ritual of the rain falling against the window, the voice of the wind, makes us remember a journey older than thought, deeper than death, a triumph, the secret ascension of love. The tasting of these things in our days and nights is the partaking of the sacrament of existence.

CECIL COLLINS

July 27

Ah midsummer!
Ripening fruits, rich vines, evening perfume,
With the waxing moon clear and full.
How the old scholars understood the transience
Of all secluded moments!

The Book of the Heart
LOY CHING-YUEN

July 28

The beauty of the trees
The softness of the air
The fragrance of the grass
Speaks to me.

The summit of the mountain
The thunder of the sky
The rhythm of the sea
Speaks to me
And my heart soars.

DAN GEORGE

July 29

This we know: the earth does not belong to man, man belongs to the earth. All things are connected like the blood which unites us all. Man did not weave the web of life, he is merely a strand in it. Whatever he does to the web, he does to himself.

CHIEF SEATTLE

July 30

Deep peace of the Running Wave to you
Deep peace of the Flowing Air to you
Deep peace of the Quiet Earth to you
Deep peace of the Shining Stars to you
Deep peace of the Gentle Night to you
Deep peace of the Son of Peace to you
Moon and Stars pour their healing light on you
Deep peace to you.

A Gaelic Blessing

July 31

I was walking in the open air on a beautiful spring morning. The wheat was growing green, the birds were singing, the dew was sparkling, the smoke rising; a transfiguring light lay over everything; this was only a tiny fragment of Earth . . . and yet the idea seemed to me not only beautiful, but also so true and obvious that she was an Angel – an Angel so sumptuous, so fresh, so like a flower and at the same time so firm and so composed, who was moving through the sky . . .

GUSTAV FECHNER

AUGUST

THE SOUL'S LIFE

I n every mystical tradition there is a certainty that we and the divine are one at the core of our being, in what we might call the soul. This soul is the prisoner of habits, desires, discursive thought and all the demanding excitements of life and it is only by connecting with it through prayer, contemplation, adoration, service of others, that we come slowly to free it and live in its supreme and healing mystery, to taste its immortality and to hear its child-like laughter.

August 1

The soul's extravagance is endless:
Spring after spring after spring . . .
We are your gardens dying,
blossoming.

RUMI

August 2

WHAT CAN WE GAIN by sailing
to the moon if we are not able to
cross the abyss that separates us
from ourselves?

The Wisdom of the Desert
THOMAS MERTON

August 3

Call the earth if you please
'The Vale of soul-making.'

Letters
JOHN KEATS

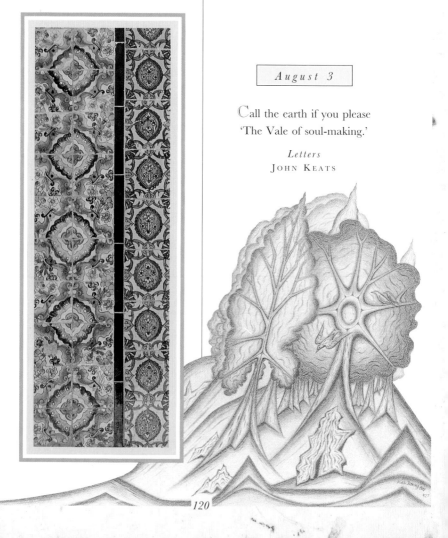

Give me my scallop-shell of quiet,
  My staff of faith to walk upon,
My scrip of joy, immortal diet,
  My bottle of salvation,
My gown of glory, hope's true gage;
And thus I'll take my pilgrimage.

Blood must be my body's balmer;
  No other balm will there be given;
Whilst my soul, like quiet palmer,
  Travelleth towards the land of heaven;
Over the silver mountains,
Where spring the nectar fountains:
    There will I kiss
    The bowl of bliss;

And drink mine everlasting fill
  Upon every milken hill.
My soul will be a-dry before;
But, after, it will thirst no more.

                    Sir Walter Raleigh

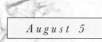

August 5

THE EVOLUTION of matter from the beginning leads to the evolution of consciousness in man; it is the universe itself which becomes conscious in man . . . It is the inner movement of the Spirit, immanent in nature, which brings about the evolution of matter and life into consciousness, and that same Spirit at work in human consciousness, latent in every man, is always at work leading to divine life.

Return to the Centre
BEDE GRIFFITHS

August 6

THE TREASURE of the Kingdom of God has been hidden by time and multiplicity and the soul's own works, or briefly by its creaturely nature. But in the measure that the soul can separate itself from this multiplicity, to that extent it reveals within itself the Kingdom of God. Here the soul and the Godhead are one . . . The whole scattered world of lower things is gathered up to oneness when the soul climbs up to that life in which there are no opposites.

MEISTER ECKHART

August 7

Our birth is but a sleep and a forgetting;
The Soul that rises with us, our life's star,
    Hath had elsewhere its setting,
    And cometh from afar;
    Not in entire forgetfulness,
    And not in utter nakedness,
But trailing clouds of glory do we come
    From God, who is our home . . .

WILLIAM WORDSWORTH

August 8

Because we have heard and because faith tells us so, we know we have souls. But we seldom consider the precious things that can be found in this soul, or who dwells within it, or its highest value.

The Interior Castle
ST. TERESA OF AVILA

August 9

Not by any travelling is the world's end reached. Verily I declare to you that within this fathom-long body with its perceptions and its mind lies the world, its arising and its ceasing and the Way that leads to its cessation.

Samyutta Nikaya
THE BUDDHA

August 10

CONSIDER our soul to be like a castle made entirely out of a diamond or of very clear crystal, in which there are many rooms.

The Interior Castle
ST. TERESA OF AVILA

August 11

There is a root or depth in thee, from whence all these faculties come forth as lines from a centre, or as branches from the body of a tree. This depth is called the centre, the fund, or bottom of the soul. This depth is the unity, the Eternity, I had almost said the infinity of thy soul, for it is so infinite that nothing can satisfy it, or give it any rest, but the infinity of God.

The Spirit of Prayer
WILLIAM LAW

August 12

GOD IS NEARER to us than our own soul. For He is the Ground in whom our Soul stands; and He is the Mean which keeps the substance and sense-nature together, so that they shall never part. For our soul sits in God in very rest; and our soul stands in God in sure strength; and our soul is kindly rooted in God in endless love. And therefore, if we want to have knowing of our Soul, and communion and loving with it, we need to seek into our God, in whom it is enclosed.

Revelations of Divine Love
JULIAN OF NORWICH

August 13

Within this earthen vessel are bowers
   and groves, and within it is the Creator:
Within this vessel are the seven oceans
   and the unnumbered stars.
The touchstone and the jewel-appraiser
   are within;
And within this vessel the Eternal
   soundeth, and the spring wells up.

KABIR

August 14

This is why the soul receives, in the highest, most secret part of its
   being, the impress of its Eternal Image, and the uninterrupted
effulgence of the divine light, and *is* the eternal dwelling-place of God:
wherein He abides as in a perpetual habitation, and yet which He
perpetually visits with the new coming and new radiance and new splendour
of His eternal birth. For where He comes, He is: and where He is,
He comes.

The Adornment of the Spiritual Marriage
JAN VAN RUYSBROECK

August 15

If the psychic entity had been from the beginning unveiled and known to its ministers, not a secluded King in a screened chamber, the human evolution would have been a rapid soul-outflowering, not the difficult, chequered and disfigured development it now is; but the veil is thick and we know not the secret Light within us, the light in the hidden crypt of the heart's innermost sanctuary.

The Life Divine
SRI AUROBINDO

August 16

O, the fabulous wings unused
Folded in the heart!

A Sleep of Prisoners
CHRISTOPHER FRY

August 17

If the doors of perception were cleansed, everything would appear to man as it is – infinite.

WILLIAM BLAKE

August 18

That fire which is the means of attaining the infinite worlds, and is also their foundation, is hidden in the sacred place of the heart.

Katha Upanishad, Part 1

I want more ideas of soul-life. I am certain that there are more yet to be found. A great life – an entire civilization – lies just outside the pale of common thought . . . A nexus of ideas exists of which nothing is known . . . a cosmos of thought. There is an Entity, a Soul-Entity, as yet unrecognized; . . . it is in addition to the existence of the soul; in addition to immortality; and beyond the idea of the deity . . . There is an immense ocean over which the mind can sail, upon which the vessel of thought has not yet been launched . . . There is so much beyond all that has ever yet been imagined.

The Story of My Heart
RICHARD JEFFERIES

As the crust of our outer nature cracks, as the walls of inner separation break down, the inner light gets through, the inner fire burns in the heart, the substance of the nature and the stuff of consciousness refine to a greater subtlety and purity, and the deeper psychic experiences . . . become possible in this subtler, purer, finer substance; the soul begins to unveil itself, the psychic personality reaches its full stature. The soul, the psychic entity, then manifests itself as the central being which upholds mind and life and body and supports all the other powers and functions of the Spirit; it takes up its greater function as the guide and ruler of the nature.

The Life Divine
SRI AUROBINDO

August 21

God's ultimate purpose is birth. He is not
content until he brings his Son to birth in us.

MEISTER ECKHART

August 22

BELIEVE in you my soul, the other I am must not abase
itself to you,
And you must not be abased to the other.
Loafe with me on the grass, loose the stop from your throat,
Not words, not music or rhyme I want, not custom or lecture,
not even the best,
Only the lull I like, the hum of your valvèd throat.

Leaves of Grass
WALT WHITMAN

August 23

THE CUP in which the world is reflected is the heart of the perfect
man. That mirror that shows reality is the heart. The heart is the
treasure of the divine mysteries. Ask the heart then, what is the purpose of
the two worlds.

LAHIJI

August 24

L ove is the true means by which the world is enjoyed: our love to others and others' love to us. We ought therefore above all things to get acquainted with the nature of love. For love is the root and foundation of nature: love is the soul of life and crown of rewards.

Centuries of Meditations
THOMAS TRAHERNE

August 25

Then was my Soul my only All to me,
A living endless Eye
Scarce bounded with the Sky
Whose Power and Act and Essence was to see;
I was an inward sphere of Light
Or an interminable Orb of Sight
Exceeding that which makes the days,
A vital Sun, that shed abroad its rays,
All Life, all Sense,
a naked, simple, pure, intelligence.

THOMAS TRAHERNE

August 26

I am a flame of fire, blazing with passionate love;
I am a spark of light, illuminating the deepest truth;
I am a rough ocean, heaving with righteous anger;
I am a calm lake, comforting the troubled breast;
I am a wild storm, raging at human sins;
I am a gentle breeze, glowing hope in the saddened heart;
I am dry dust, choking wordly ambition;
I am wet earth, bearing rich fruits of grace.

The Black Book of Carmarthan

August 27

The seed of God is in us. Given an intelligent and hard-working farmer, it will thrive and grow up to God, whose seed it is; and accordingly its fruits will be God-nature. Pear seeds grow into pear trees, nut seeds into nut trees, and God seed into God.

MEISTER ECKHART

Not I, not I, but the wind that blows through me!
A fine wind is blowing, the new direction of Time.
If only I let it bear me, carry me, if only it carry me!
If only I am sensitive, subtle, Oh delicate, a
        winged gift!
If only, most lovely of all, I yield myself and am
        borrowed
By the fine, fine wind that takes its course through
        the chaos of the world
Like a fine, an exquisite chisel, a wedge blade
        inserted;
If only I am keen and hard like the sheer tip
        of a wedge
Driven by invisible blows,
The rock will split, we shall come at the wonder, we
        shall find the Hesperides.
Oh, for the wonder that bubbles into my soul;
I would be a good fountain, a good well-head,
Would blur no whisper, spoil no expression.

❧

What is the knocking?
What is the knocking at the door in the night?
It is somebody wants to do us harm.

❧

No, no, it is the three strange angels.
    Admit them, admit them.

The Song of the Man Who has Come Through
D.H. LAWRENCE

131

August 29

AND MY LETTER, my awakener,
I found before me on the road;
And as with its Voice it had awakened me,
So too with its Light it was leading me,
Shining before me in a garment of radiance,
Glistening like royal silk.
And with its Voice and its guidance,
It also encouraged me to speed,
And with his Love was drawing me on.

Hymn of the Robe of Glory
BARDESANES

August 30

How could the soul not take flight
When from the glorious presence
A soft call flows sweet as honey, comes right up to her
And whispers, 'Rise up now, come away.'

RUMI

August 31

ar from the daily accident,
The false reality, I wake:
Thunder and sweetness fill the cup,
Strong plumes and jewels in my hair.

Unpublished Poems
LEWIS THOMPSON

SEPTEMBER

THE ALCHEMY OF JOY

The heart is an umbilical cord which connects us to the Ground of Being. The heart is our creative imagination, born of our instinct for relationship with this Divine Ground. The heart generates all our quests, all our hopes and longings and will ultimately bring us to reunion with this Ground. Without the heart, without the instinct to feel, to imagine, to hope and to love, life is meaningless, sterile, dead. When we are in touch with our heart, it comes alive, it vibrates, it sings.

The spiritual life is the uncovering of deeper and deeper levels of joy until that joy that streams from the god-head itself is realized and known in every breath. Every increase in joy is an increase in strength and peace of soul and an increase in all the powers of creativity that reveal life as a divine dance. As Sohrawardi, the great Persian mystic said, 'God has given us all a garden in this world, and when you have come into it and into your true joy, you will long for no other garden, and no other world.'

September 1

Oh, light eternal, who
only abides in yourself, only
yourself can comprehend and, of
yourself comprehended and
yourself comprehending,
do love and smile.

Paradiso, Canto 33
DANTE

September 2

AN EYE is meant to see
things. The soul is here
for its own joy.

RUMI

September 3

On the day of liberation you
will laugh but what is on the
day of laughter is also now.

SRI RAMANA MAHARSHI

September 4

Your whole body must be
united in laughter . . . you
should shake with merriment
from head to foot . . . I want you
to laugh with your whole heart
and soul, with all the breath of
life . . . you will see how the
laughter that comes from such a
heart defeats the world.

Teachings
SRI ANANDA MAYI MA

September 5

W hen God laughs at the soul and the soul laughs back at God, the persons of the Trinity are born. To speak in hyperbole, when the Father laughs to the Son and the Son laughs back to the Father, that laughter gives pleasure, that pleasure gives joy, that joy gives love, and love gives the persons (of the Trinity) in which the Holy Spirit is one.

MEISTER ECKHART

September 6

September 7

L OVE swims in the sea of joy, that is the sea of delight, the stream of divine influences.

The Mirror of Simple Souls

September 8

Beauty saves. Beauty heals. Beauty motivates. Beauty unites. Beauty returns us to our origins, and here lies the ultimate act of saving, of healing, of overcoming dualism. Beauty allows us to forget the pain and dwell on the joy.

Original Blessing
MATTHEW FOX

The lover of God flies and runs and rejoices, is free and can be held by nothing.

The Imitation of Christ
THOMAS À KEMPIS

137

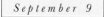

September 9

T̲o obtain a vision of Beauty and Divinity, each man should begin by making himself beautiful and divine.

Ennead 1, vi
PLOTINUS

September 10

W̲e of the here and now are not for a moment hedged in by the time-world, nor confined within it . . . we are incessantly flowing over and over to those who preceded us . . . We are the bees of the invisible. We deliriously gather the honey of the visible, to accumulate it in the great golden hive of the invisible.

Letters
RAINER MARIA RILKE

September 11

I̲ am certain of nothing but of the holiness of the Heart's affections and the truth of Imagination. What the imagination seizes as Beauty must be truth.

Letters
JOHN KEATS

September 12

L̲OVE raises the spirit above the sphere of reverence and worship into one of laughter and dalliance.

COVENTRY PATMORE

September 13

Where there is creation there is progress.
Where there is no creation there is no progress:
Know the nature of creation.
Where there is joy there is creation.
Where there is no joy there is no creation:
Know the nature of joy.
Where there is the Infinite there is joy.
There is no joy in the finite.

Chandogya Upanishad

September 14

It dances today my heart, like a
    Peacock it dances.
It sports a mosaic of passions
    Like a peacock's tail,
It soars to the sky with delight, it
    quests, O wildly,
It dances today, my heart, like a
    peacock it dances.

New Rain
RABINDRANATH TAGORE

September 15

There is the path of joy and
there is the path of pleasure. Both
attract the soul . . . The two paths
lie in front of man. Pondering on
them, the wise man chooses the
path of joy; the fool takes the
path of pleasure.

Katha Upanishad

September 16

B eing an artist means, not reckoning and counting, but ripening like the tree which does not force its sap and stands confident in the storms of spring without the fear that after them may come no summer. It does come. But it comes only to the patient, who are there as though eternity lay before them, so unconcernedly still and wide . . . Patience is everything.

Letters to a Young Poet
RAINER MARIA RILKE

September 17

The secret of life is to share the creative madness of God.

AN ENGLISH MYSTIC

September 18

Effortlessly
Love flows from God into man,
Like a bird
Who rivers the air
Without moving her wings.
Thus we move in His world
One in body and soul,
Though outwardly separate in form.
As the Source strikes the note,
Humanity sings –
The Holy Spirit is our harpist,
And all strings
Which are touched in Love
Must sound.

The Flowing Light of the Godhead
MECHTHILD OF MAGDEBURG

September 19

There is a poem
at the heart of things.

WALLACE STEVENS

September 20

There is in all things an inexhaustible sweetness and purity, a silence that is a fountain of action and joy. It rises up in wordless gentleness and flows out to me from unseen roots of all created being.

THOMAS MERTON

September 21

The psalm reads: 'For singing to our God is good.'
Rabbi Elimeleckh expounded this: 'It is good if man can bring about that God sings within him.'

Tales of the Hasidim

September 22

Dive deep, O mind into the ocean of Divine Beauty. You will discover a new gem instant after instant.

SRI RAMAKRISHNA

September 23

I SLEEP, but my heart waketh:
it is the voice of my beloved that knocketh, saying:
Open to me, my sister, my love, my dove, my undefiled;
for my head is filled with dew,
and my locks with the drops of the night.

Song of Songs 5:2

September 24

When the moon rises in the Heart of Heaven
And a light breeze touches the mirror-like surface of the lake,
That is indeed a moment of pure joy.
But few are they who are aware of it.

TAOIST SAGE

September 25

Whatever gladdens the mind is
of the scent of the Beloved,
Whatever enraptures the heart is
a ray from my friend.

RUMI

September 26

Lately I became aware of the meaning of Quietude.
Day after day I stayed away from the multitude.
I cleaned my cottage and prepared it for the visit of a monk
Who came to me from the distant mountains.
He descended from the cloud-hidden peaks
To see me in my thatched house.
Sitting in the grass we shared the resin of the pine.
Burning incense we read the sutras of Tao.
When the day was over we lighted our lamp.
The temple bells announced the beginning of the evening.
Suddenly I realized that Quietude is indeed Joy,
And I felt that my life has abundant leisure.

WANG WEI

September 27

Oh daylight rise! Atoms are dancing,
Souls, lost in ecstasy, are dancing,
I'll whisper in your ear where the dance will take you.
All atoms in the air, in the desert,
They are all like madmen; each atom, happy or miserable,
Is passionate for the Sun of which nothing can be said.

RUMI

September 28

The heart of men has been so made by God that, like a flint, it contains a hidden fire which is evolved by music and harmony, and renders man beside himself with ecstasy. These harmonies are echoes of that higher world of reality which we call the world of spirits . . . they fan into a flame whatever love is already dormant in the heart.

AL-GHAZZALI

September 29

I n the transformation of his mind the calligrapher borrows the brush. It is not the brush that works the miracle. The transformation can only take place when the mind is tranquil and penetrates into the utmost subtlety. Thus spirit responds and mind is transparent. This is similar to plucking the harp; silken sounds and subtle melodies are produced at ease.

Treatise on the Marrow of the Brush
YU SHIH-NAN

September 30

T hen, set free from the worlds of sense and of intellect, the soul enters into the mysterious obscurity of a holy ignorance, and . . . loses itself in him who can be neither seen nor apprehended . . . Then the soul comes to know a special joy: fruition or the touch divine.

On The Mystical Theology and The Divine Names
DIONYSIUS THE AREOPAGITE

OCTOBER

THE HEART IS NOTHING BUT THE SEA OF LIGHT:
THE MYSTIC EXPERIENCE

eister Eckhart says that fire transforms all things it touches into its own nature. When at last we enter the fire of the authentic mystical experience, we enter into the ultimate alchemical process, one in which, slowly, over many years of constantly re-entering that fire of vision and divine love, we transmute all that is dark and unconscious in us into love; and all that is wounded and negative in us into a sacred passion of creative service, in all the different ways we may be called to express it.

October 1

The heart is nothing but the
Sea of Light . . .
the place of the vision of God.

RUMI

October 2

And I entered and beheld
with the eye of my soul
(such as it was) above the same
eye of my soul, above my mind,
the Light Unchangeable . . . . He
that knows the Truth knows what
that Light is, and he that knows
It, knows eternity.

Confessions, Book VII
ST. AUGUSTINE

October 3

Here there is nothing but
an eternal seeing and staring at
that Light, by that Light, and in
that Light.

*The Adornment of the
Spiritual Marriage*
JAN VAN RUYSBROECK

October 4

WHO SAYS that Spirit is not
known, knows; who claims that
he knows, knows nothing. The
ignorant think that Spirit lies
within knowledge; the wise man
knows It beyond knowledge.
Spirit is known through
revelation. The living man who
finds Spirit, finds Truth.

Kena Upanishad

October 5

The day of my spiritual awakening
was the day I saw – and knew I saw –
all things in God and God in all things.

The Flowing Light of the Godhead
MECHTHILD OF MAGDEBUR

October 6

THE EYES OF MY SOUL were opened, and I beheld the plenitude of
God, wherein I did comprehend the whole world, both here and beyond the
sea, and the abyss and ocean and all things. In all these things I beheld
naught save the divine power, in a manner assuredly indescribable, so that
through excess of marvelling the soul cried with a loud voice, saying 'This
whole world is full of God!' Wherefore I comprehended how small a thing is
the whole world . . . and that the Power of God exceeds and fills all. Then
he said unto me: 'I have shown thee something of My Power . . . Behold
now My humility.' Then I was given an insight into the deep humility of
God towards man. And comprehending that unspeakable power and
beholding that deep humility, my soul marvelled greatly, and did esteem
itself to be nothing at all.

ANGELA OF FOLIGNO

October 7

And in this He showed me something small, no bigger than a hazelnut, lying in the palm of my hand . . . as round as a ball. I looked at it with the eye of my understanding and thought: What can this be? I was amazed that it could last, for I thought that because of its littleness it would suddenly have fallen into nothing. And I was answered in my understanding: It lasts and always will, because God loves it; and thus everything has being through the love of God.

Revelations of Divine Love
JULIAN OF NORWICH

October 8

I see without eyes, and I hear without ears. I feel without feeling and taste without tasting. I know neither form nor measure; for without seeing I yet behold an operation so divine that the words I first used, perfection, purity, and the like, seem to me now mere lies in the presence of truth . . . Nor can I any longer say, 'My God, my all.' Everything is mine, for all that is God's seems to be wholly mine. I am mute and lost in God.

ST. CATHERINE OF GENOA

October 9

This is a supernatural thing, which we cannot obtain by any effort on our part. The soul rests in peace . . . all (her) powers are at rest. The soul understands, with an understanding quite different from that given by the external senses, that she is now quite close to God and that, if she drew just a little nearer, she would become one thing with Him by union. She does not see Him with eyes of the body or the soul . . . The soul understands He is here, though not so clearly. She does not know herself how she understands; she sees only that she is in the Kingdom . . .

The Way of Perfection
ST. TERESA OF AVILA

October 10

Fire transforms all things it touches into its own nature. The wood does not change the fire into itself, but the fire changes the wood into itself. In the same way we are transformed into God so that we may know him as he is. Acting and becoming are one. God and I are one in this work; he acts and I become.

MEISTER ECKHART

October 11

Wouldst thou know my meaning?
Lie down in the Fire
See and taste the Flowing
Godhead through thy being;
Feel the Holy Spirit
Moving and compelling
Thee within the Flowing
Fire and Light of God.

*The Flowing Light
of the Godhead*
MECHTHILD OF MAGDEBURG

Too late came I to love thee, O thou Beauty both so ancient and so fresh, Yea, too late came I to love thee. And behold, thou were within me, and I out of myself, where I made search for thee.

Confessions, Book X
ST. AUGUSTINE

Suddenly I was wrapped in gentleness, there was a blinding flash, then a diaphanous light in the likeness of a human being. I watched attentively and there he was . . . He came towards me, greeting me so kindly that my bewilderment faded and my alarm gave way to a feeling of familiarity. And then I began to complain to him of the trouble I had with this problem of knowledge.

'Awaken to youself,' he said to me, 'and your problem will be solved.'

The Wisdom of Illumination
SOHRAWARDI

And so it came . . . It tiptoed itself into my heart, silently, imperceptibly, and I looked at it with wonder. It was a still, small, light-blue flame, trembling softly. It had the infinite sweetness of a first love, like an offering of fragrant flowers with gentle hands, the heart full of stillness and wonder and peace.

Daughter of Fire
IRINA TWEEDIE

October 15

I CONCERNED MYSELF to remember God, to know Him, to love Him and to seek Him. When I had come to the end I saw that He had remembered me before I had remembered Him, that His knowledge of me had preceded my knowledge of Him, that His love towards me had existed before my love to Him and He had sought me before I sought Him.

BISTAMI

October 16

He has awaited me for countless ages,
for love of me He has lost His heart:
Yet I did not know the bliss that was so near to me,
for my love was not yet awake.

KABIR

October 17

If the soul knows God in creatures, night falls. If it sees how they have their being in God, morning breaks. But if it sees the Being that is in God himself alone, it is high noon! See! This is what one ought to desire with mad fervour – that all his life should become Being.

MEISTER ECKHART

October 18

October 19

Then the soul neither sees, nor distinguishes by seeing, nor imagines that there are two things: but becomes as it were another thing, ceases to be itself and belong to itself. It belongs to God and is one with Him, like two concentric circles: concurring they are One; but when they separate they are two . . . Since in this conjunction with the Deity there were not two things, but the perceiver was one with the perceived . . .

Ennead VI,9
PLOTINUS

To be of heaven is to be in Tao.
Tao is forever and he
that possesses it,
Though his body ceases,
is not destroyed.

Tao Teh King
LAO TZU

October 20

Under the rich, self-dreaming mango-spires
Scented like satyr loves and milky seas,
The frozen spiky foam of moonlight fires,
Falls to the core of earth an indigo night of leaves.

The naked heart of love, rich, simple, rare,
unmeasured sweetness, grave, most delicate,
In golden plumes dusk with redoubled light
Given over beyond recall upon the common air.

An amber cloud deepens to secrecy
So open a dream its heaven eludes the sense –
And all that rapture, all that ecstasy
Becomes its own pure angel, mute with radiance.

Unpublished Poems
LEWIS THOMPSON

October 21

All seemed a world in flower,
and I was the soul of this world.

MARAGALL

October 22

The infinite dwelling of the Infinite Being
is everywhere: in earth, water, sky and air:
Firm as the thunderbolt, the seat of the seeker
is established above the void.
He who is within is without: I see Him and none else.

KABIR

October 23

I was utterly alone with the sun and the earth. Lying down on the grass, I spoke in my soul to the earth, the sun, the air, and the distant sea far beyond sight. I thought of the earth's firmness – I felt it bear me up; through the grassy couch there came an influence as if I could feel the great earth speaking to me . . . Touching the crumble of earth, the blade of grass, the thyme flower, breathing the earth-encircling air, thinking of the sea and the sky, holding out my hand for the sunbeams to touch it, prone on the sward in token of deep reverence, thus I prayed that I might touch to the unutterable existence infinitely higher than deity.

The Story of My Heart
RICHARD JEFFERIES

October 24

I seemed alone with immensity, and there came at last that
melting of the divine darkness into the life within me
for which I prayed.

Song and Its Fountains
A.E.

October 25

From about half past ten in the evening to
about half an hour after midnight. Fire.
God of Abraham, God of Isaac, God of Jacob,
Not the God of philosophers and scholars.
Absolute Certainty: Beyond Reason, Joy. Peace.
Forgetfulness of the world and everything but God.
The world has not known thee, but I have known thee,
Joy! joy! joy! tears of joy!

BLAISE PASCAL

October 26

When Rabbi Elimelekh said the Prayer of Sanctification on the sabbath, he occasionally took out his watch and looked at it. For in that hour, his soul threatened to dissolve in bliss, and so he looked at his watch in order to steady himself in Time and the world.

Tales of the Hasidim

October 27

It is the time of union,
It is the time of vision,
It is the time of resurrection,
It is the time of grace,
It is the time of generosity,
The treasure of gifts has arrived.
The brilliance of the sea has flashed forth.
The dawn of blessing has arisen
What is this ancient wisdom
The source of these living waters is in your head
and in your eyes.

RUMI

October 28

Mine – by the Right of the White Election!
Mine – by the Royal Seal!
Mine – by the Sign in the Scarlet prison –
Bars – cannot conceal!
Mine – here – in Vision – and in Veto!
Mine – by the Grave's Repeal –
Delirious Charter!
Mine – long as Ages steal!

EMILY DICKINSON

October 29

I am neither the mind, the intellect,
   nor the whispering voice within;
Neither the eyes, the ears, the nose,
   nor the mouth.
I am not water, fire, earth, nor ether –
I am Consciousness and Bliss.
   I am Shiva! I am Shiva!

SHANKARACHARYA

October 30

Cloud pregnant with a million bolts of lightning,
   Love gives birth to the philosopher's stone.
   My soul is flooded by your Sea of splendor,
   Being and cosmos drown there silently.

RUMI

October 31

Abbot Lot came to Abbot Joseph and said, Father, according as I am able, I keep my little rule and my little fast, my prayer, meditation and contemplative silence: and according as I am able, I strive to cleanse my heart of thought: now what more should I do? The Elder rose up in reply and stretched out his hands to heaven, and his fingers became ten lamps of fire. He said: Why not be totally changed into fire?

The Wisdom of the Desert
THOMAS MERTON

NOVEMBER

TO CHOOSE IS TO BE EMPOWERED

Our unwillingness to face the extremity of the situation that confronts the entire human race is part of the problem. We are certainly at the end of a civilization, the end of a whole cycle of history. The facts of our global crisis – a crisis that is at once political and economic, psychological and environmental – show us clearly that the human race has no hope of survival unless it chooses to undergo a total change of heart, a massive, quite unprecedented spiritual transformation. Only the leap into a new consciousness can engender the vision, moral passion, joy and energy necessary to effect change on the scale and with the self-sacrifice necessary to save the planet in the time we have. The message we are being sent by history can be summed up in four words: transform or die out. Many experts agree that we have, at the most, fifteen or twenty years left before extreme crisis becomes unalterable catastrophe. Human survival depends on whether we are brave enough to face the full desolation of what we have done to our psyches and the planet, and wise and humble enough to turn to the Divine inside and outside us to learn what we will need to go forward.

Bede Griffiths, just before he died, said, 'The hour of God and mankind's greatest ordeal is now here. Everything depends on whether we can abandon our pride before it is too late.'

November 1

The human heart can go the lengths of God.
   Dark and cold we may be, but this
Is no winter now. The frozen misery
   Of centuries breaks, cracks, begins to move;
The thunder is the thunder of the floes,
   The thaw, the flood, the upstart Spring.
Thank God our time is now when wrong
   Comes up to face us everywhere.
Never to leave us till we take
   The longest stride of soul men ever took.
Affairs are now soul size,
   The enterprise
Is exploration into God.
   Where are you making for? It takes
So many thousand years to wake
   But will you wake for pity's sake?

A Sleep of Prisoners
CHRISTOPHER FRY

November 2

HUMANITY is being taken to the point where it will have to choose between suicide and adoration.

Letters
TEILHARD DE CHARDIN

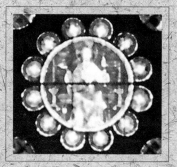

November 3

The world today hangs on a single thread, and that thread is the psyche of man.

C.G. JUNG

November 4

In the turmoil of our time, we are being called to a new order of reality. Working toward that consciousness, we suffer, but our suffering opens us to the wounds of the world and the love that can heal.

Leaving My Father's House
MARION WOODMAN

November 5

There is a lamentable departure of divinity from man, when nothing worthy of heaven, or celestial concerns, is heard or believed, and when every divine voice is by a necessary silence dumb.

HERMES TRISMEGISTUS

November 6

We are without cosmos, without myth, without ritual worthy of the name. No wonder we are cosmically sad, cosmically lonely, cosmically destructive in our military plans to rain death on the rest of creation we know.

Original Blessing
MATTHEW FOX

November 7

The makers of images
Dwell with us still
We must listen
To their speech
Re-learn their
Songs
Recharge the psychic
Interspaces
Of our dying
Age
Or live dumb
And blind
Devoid of old
Song
Divorced from
The great dreams
Of the magical and fearful
Universe.

Lament of the Images
An African Elegy
BEN OKRI

November 8

THE DIVINE and the demonic are very close together; only a thin line separates them/us. We who are indeed capable of divinity are also capable of the demonic. And the deepest of all demonic activity is the use of our divine imaginations to invent destruction.

Original Blessing
MATTHEW FOX

November 9

any stories have been heard
that the sun will go out,
the world will come to an end.
But if we all act well and think well it will not end.
That is why we are still looking after
the sun and the moon and the land.

THE KOGIS

November 10

If the dynamics of the universe from the beginning shaped the course of the heavens, lighted the sun, and formed the earth, if this same dynamism brought forth the continents and the seas and atmosphere, if it awakened life in the primordial cell and then brought into being the unnumbered variety of living beings, and finally brought us into being and guided us safely through the turbulent centuries, there is reason to believe that this same guiding process is precisely what has awakened in us our present understanding of ourselves and our relation to this stupendous process. Sensitized to such guidance from the very structure and functioning of the universe, we can have confidence in the future that awaits the human adventure.

The Dream of the Earth
THOMAS BERRY

November 11

Where danger is there rises the saving one also.

HOELDERLIN

November 12

The driving impulse of the West's masculine consciousness has been its dialectical quest not only to realize itself, to forge its own autonomy but also, finally, to recover its connection with the whole, to come to terms with the great feminine principle in life: to differentiate itself from but then rediscover and reunite with the feminine, with the mystery of life, of nature, of soul.

The Passion of the Western Mind
RICHARD TARNAS

November 13

The eternal feminine is thrusting her way into contemporary consciousness. Shekinah, Kwan Yin, Sophia, whatever her name, she is the manifestation of the divine in matter.

Leaving My Father's House
MARION WOODMAN

November 14

When a forest is on fire
A gale will only fan the flame.
It certainly will not blow it out.
So for a Boddhisattva who has
received instruction
all catastrophic situations can
be taken onto the path.

DILGO KHYENTSE

November 15

When all the world is filled
with evils
place all setbacks on the path
of Liberation.

ATISHA

November 16

Now is the time when your
action is practise.

THE DALAI LAMA

T he non-violent approach does not immediately change the heart of the oppressor. It first does something to the hearts and souls of those committed to it. It gives them a new self-respect; it calls up resources of strength and courage that they did not know they had. Finally, it reaches the opponent and so stirs his conscience that reconciliation becomes a reality.

MARTIN LUTHER KING, JR.

For in truth, in this world, hatred is not appeased by hatred. Hatred is appeased by love alone. This is the eternal law.

DHAMMAPADA

My religion is to have nothing
to be ashamed of when I die.

MILAREPA

Under the sword lifted high
There is hell, making you tremble
But go ahead,
And you have the land of bliss.

MIYAMOTO MUSASHI

Fear not, for I have redeemed
you, I have called you by
your name; you are mine. When
you pass through the waters, I
will be with you; and through the
rivers, they shall not overwhelm
you; when you walk through fire
you shall not be burned, and the
flame will not consume you.

Isaiah 43:2

The truly wise person
kneels at the feet of all creatures
and is not afraid to endure
the mockery of others.

MECHTHILD OF MAGDEBURG

November 23

L ord, make me an instrument
Of thy peace, where there is hatred,
Let me sow love;
Where there is injury, pardon;
Where there is doubt, faith;
Where there is despair, hope;
Where there is darkness, light;
And where there is sadness, joy.
O Divine Master, grant that
I may not so much seek
To be consoled as to console;
To be understood as to understand;
To be loved as to love;
For it is in giving that we receive,
It is in forgiving that we
Are forgiven, and it is in dying
That we are born to eternal life.

Prayer of St. Francis

November 24

O LOVE, O pure deep love, be
  here, be now
Be all; worlds dissolve into your
  stainless endless radiance,
Frail living leaves burn with you
  brighter than cold stars:
Make me your servant, your
  breath, your core.

RUMI

November 25

For as long as space exists
And sentient beings endure,
  May I too remain,
To dispel the misery of the world.

SHANTIDEVA

November 26

We all long for heaven where God
is, but we have it in our power to be
in heaven with Him at this very
moment. But being happy with Him
now means:

Loving as He loves,
Helping as He helps,
Giving as He gives,
Serving as He serves,
Rescuing as He rescues,
Being with Him twenty-four hours,
Touching Him in His
  distressing disguise.

MOTHER TERESA

November 27

To give our Lord a perfect
hospitality, Mary and Martha
must combine.

The Interior Castle
ST. TERESA OF AVILA

November 28

IF YOU FOLLOW your bliss you put yourself on a kind of track that has
been there all the while, waiting for you, and the life that you ought to be
living is the one you are living. When you can see that, you begin to meet
people who are in the field of your bliss, and they open the doors to you. I
say follow your bliss and don't be afraid and doors will open where you
didn't know they were going to be.

The Power of Myth
JOSEPH CAMPBELL

| November 29 | November 30 |

Because everything we do and everything we are is in jeopardy, and because the peril is immediate and unremitting, every person is the right person to act and every moment is the right moment to begin.

JONATHAN SCHELL

It's not the earthquake
that controls
The advent of a different life
But storms of generosity
And visions of incandescent souls.

BORIS PASTERNAK

DECEMBER

THE SACRED MARRIAGE

With the sacred marriage we return to where we started and know the place for the first time; know that everything we are, and think and do springs always from the Divine Ground and falls back into the Divine Essence. Life is then lived naturally as a completely sacred experience where all the old barriers between body and spirit, heaven and earth, life and death, are dissolved into an inexpressible experience of union, peace and joy.

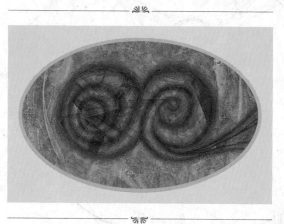

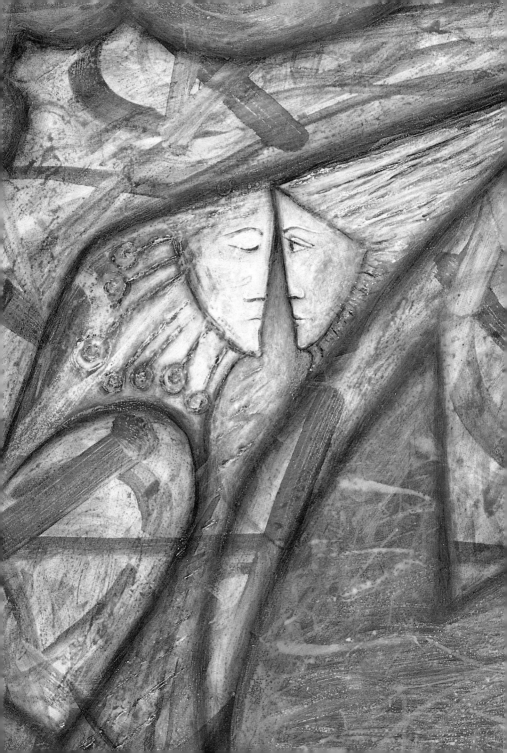

December 1

ise up, my love, my fair one, and come away.
For lo, the winter is past,
the rain is over and gone;
The flowers appear on the earth;
the time of the singing of birds is come,
And the voice of the turtle is heard in our land;
The fig tree putteth forth her green figs,
and the vines with the tender grapes
give a good smell.
Arise, my love, my fair one, and come away.

Song of Songs 2:10-13

December 2

hen love has carried us above and beyond all things, into the Divine Dark . . . we receive in peace the Incomprehensible Light, enfolding us and penetrating us . . . What is this Light, if it be not a contemplation of the Infinite, and an intuition of Eternity? We behold that which we are, and we are that which we behold; because our thought, life and being are uplifted in simplicity and made one with the Divine Truth which is God.

The Sparkling Stone
JAN VAN RUYSBROECK

176

December 3

Ascend with great intelligence from earth to heaven and again descend to earth, and unite together the powers of higher things with lower things. Thus you will receive the glory of the whole world and darkness will fly about from you.

HERMES TRISMEGISTUS

December 4

Beauty will come in the dawn
And beauty will come with the sunlight.
Beauty will come to us from everywhere,
Where heaven ends, where the sky ends.
Beauty will surround us. We walk in beauty.

BILLY YELLOW
NAVAJO MEDICINE MAN

December 5

As for the state of the saints, it is
warm and shining because the
saints live and walk in full noon.

JAN VAN RUYSBROECK

December 6

FOR THOSE who have become the children of light, and sons and daughters of the Day which is to come, for those who walk at all times in the light, the day of the Lord will never come, for they are always with God and in God.

ST. SYMEON

December 7

Unity is this: that a man feel himself to be gathered together with all his powers in the unity of his heart. Unity brings inward peace and restfulness of heart. Unity of heart is a bond which draws together body and soul, heart and senses, and all the outward and inward powers and encloses them in the union of love.

The Adornment of the Spiritual Marriage
JAN VAN RUYSBROECK

December 8

The third and highest degree of tawhid (the unity of God) is the one that God has chosen for Himself, the one of which He alone is worthy; and He radiates from it a ray of light in the consciousness of a group of His chosen ones, while causing them to be silent about defining it and helpless to transmit it.

AL-HALLAJ

December 9

Deep has called unto deep
and all things have vanished
into unity.
The waves and the ocean have
become one.
Nothing can come,
and nothing can now pass away.

TUKARAM

December 10

I have put duality away,
I have seen the two worlds are one;
One I seek, One I know,
One I see, One I call.
He is the first, He is the last,
He is the outward, he is the inward.

RUMI

December 11

When the inward and the outward are illumined, and all is clear, you are one with the light of sun and moon. When developed to its ultimate state, this is a round luminosity which nothing can deceive, the subtle body of a unified spirit, pervading the whole universe. Then you have the same function as the sun and moon.

Awakening to the Tao
LIU I-MING

December 12

When one begins to apply this magic, it is as if, in the middle of one's being, there were a non-being. When in the course of time the work is finished, and beyond the body there is another body, it is as if, in the middle of the non-being, there were a being. Only after a completed work of a hundred days will the Light be real, then only will it become spirit-fire. After a hundred days, there develops by itself in the middle of the Light, a point of the true Light-pole. Suddenly there develops the seed pearl. It is as if man and woman embraced and a conception took place.

The Secret of the Golden Flower

December 13

Yin and Yang arise, alternating over and over again,
Everywhere producing the sound of thunder.
White clouds assemble on the summit,
Sweet dew bathes the polar mountain.
Having drunk the wine of longevity,
You wander free; who can know you?

The Hundred Character Tablet
Lu Yen

December 14

Whom you make the two one,
and when you make the inner as the outer
and the outer as the inner
and the above as the below,
and when you make the male and female
into a single one,
so that the male will not be male
and the female not be female . . .
then shall you enter the Kingdom.

The Gospel according to Thomas, logion 22

December 15

He who is in the sun,
and in the fire,
and in the heart of man
is One.
He who knows this is
one with the One.

Svetasvatara Upanishad

December 16

The spiritual marriage may also be compared to water falling from the sky into a river or fountain, where the waters are united, and it would no longer be possible to divide them, or to separate the water of the river from that which has fallen from the heavens.

The Interior Castle
ST. TERESA OF AVILA

December 17

I and my Father are one.

JOHN 10:30

December 18

When the I am myself goes, the I am all comes. When the I am all goes, the I am comes. When even I am goes, Reality alone is and in it every I am is preserved and glorified.

I Am That
SRI NISARGADATTA MAHARAJ

December 19

And when That is seen in its immanence and transcendence then the ties that have bound the heart are unloosened, the doubts of the mind vanish, and the law of karma works no more.

Mundaka Upanishad

December 20

I have stilled my restless mind, and my heart is radiant:
for in Thatness I have seen beyond Thatness,
in company I have seen the Comrade Himself.
Living in bondage, I have set myself free:
I have broken away from the clutch of all narrowness.
Kabir says: 'I have attained the unattainable,
and my heart is coloured with the colour of love.'

KABIR

December 21

When there is one, there is
stability: with two, there is
contention. When the jade is in
the mountain, the plants and trees
are verdant: when the pearls grow
in the depths, the riverbanks do
not wither.

Awakening to the Tao
LIU I-MING

December 22

No other love is like unto the
ecstasy of the moment when spirit
cleaves to spirit and becomes
one – one love.

THE ZOHAR

December 23

*G*lorious is the moment we sit in the palace, you and I
Two forms, two faces, but a single soul, you and I
The flowers will blaze and bird cries shower us with immortality
The moment we enter the garden, you and I . . .
What a miracle, you and I, one love, one lover, one Fire
In this world and the next, in an ecstasy without end.

RUMI

December 24

I found him whom my soul loveth:
I held him, and would not let him go . . .
I am my beloved's, and my beloved is mine.

Song of Songs 6:3

December 25

The image of the Beloved suddenly
lifted its head from the heart.
Like the moon from the horizon, like a
flower from a branch.

RUMI

December 26

Oh, night that guided me,
Oh, night more lovely than the dawn,
Oh, night that joined Beloved with lover,
Lover transformed in the Beloved!
All ceased and I abandoned myself,
Leaving my cares forgotten among the lilies.

Dark Night of the Soul
ST. JOHN OF THE CROSS

December 27

nd the coming of the Bridegroom is so swift that he is perpetually coming and dwelling within with unfathomable riches, and ever coming anew in His Person, without interception, with such new brightness that it seems as though he had never come before. For His coming consists beyond time, in an eternal Now, which is ever received with new longings and new joy. Behold, the delight and the joy which the Bridegroom brings with Him in the coming are boundless and without measure, for they are Himself.

The Adornment of the Spiritual Marriage
JAN VAN RUYSBROECK

December 28

Oh wonder of wonders! When I think of the union
of the soul with God! . . . The divine love-spring
surges over the soul, sweeping her out of herself into
the unnamed being of her original source . . . In this
exalted state she has lost her proper self and is
flowing full-flood into the unity of the divine
nature . . . Henceforth I shall not speak about the
soul, for she has lost her name in the oneness of
the divine essence. There she is no more
called soul: she is called infinite being.

from Tractate 11
MEISTER ECKHART

187

December 29

Love bade me welcome: yet my soul drew back,
  Guiltie of dust and sinne.
But quick-ey'd Love, observing me grow slack
  From my first entrance in,
Drew nearer to me, sweetly questioning
  If I lack'd any thing.

'A guest,' I answered, 'worthy to be here':
  Love said, 'You shall be he.'
'I the unkinde, ungratefull? Ah, my deare,
  I cannot look on thee.'
Love took my hand, and smiling did reply,
  'Who made the eyes but I?'

'Truth Lord, but I have marr'd them: let my shame
  Go where it doth deserve.'
'And know you not, says Love, 'who bore the blame?'
  'My deare, then I will serve.'
'You must sit down,' says Love, 'And taste my meat':
  So I did sit and eat.

GEORGE HERBERT

December 30

He brought me to the
banqueting house,
and his banner over me
was love.

Song of Songs 2:4

December 31

Ye shall know the truth
and the truth shall make you free.

JOHN 8:32

The compilers and publishers gratefully acknowledge the following sources for permission to use copyright material. Every effort has been made to trace the copyright holders. Some quotations have been noted down without references during the last forty years and cannot now be traced. The compilers and publishers would be grateful to hear from any copyright holders not acknowledged.

Ballantine Books. Excerpt from THE PASSION OF THE WESTERN MIND by Richard Tarnas, Ballantine Books, New York, 1991. Copyright © 1991 Richard Tarnas. Reprinted by kind permission of the author.

Bantam Doubleday Dell Publishing Group Inc. Excerpts from THE POWER OF MYTH by Joseph Campbell with Bill Moyers. Doubleday 1988, New York. Reprinted by kind permission of Bantam Doubleday Dell Publishing Group Inc. Excerpts from TWO SUNS RISING by Jonathan Star. Translation copyright © 1992 by Jonathan Star. Used by permission of Bantam Books, a division of Bantam Doubeday Dell Publishing Group Inc. Excerpt from A GARDEN BEYOND PARADISE by Rumi; Jonathan Star & Shahram Shiva. Translation copyright © 1992 by Jonathan Star. Used by permission of Bantam Books, a division of Bantam Doubleday Dell Publishing Group Inc.

Bear & Co., Inc., selected excerpts from ORIGINAL BLESSING by Matthew Fox. Copyright © 1983, BEAR AND CO., INC., P.O. Box 2860, NM 87504. Reprinted by permission of the publishers.

The Belknap Press of Harvard University Press. Excerpts from THE POEMS OF EMILY DICKINSON, Thomas H. Johnson, ed., Cambridge, Mass.: The Belknap Press of Harvard University Press. Copyright © 1951, 1955, 1979, 1983 by the President and Fellows of Harvard College. Reprinted by kind permission of the publishers and the Trustees of Amherst College. (Published in WOMEN IN PRAISE OF THE SACRED by Jane Hirshfield.).

Blue Dolphin Publishing. Excerpt from DAUGHTER OF FIRE: A DIARY OF A SPIRITUAL TRAINING WITH A SUFI MASTER by Irina Tweedie. Blue Dolphin Publishing, 1986, Nevada City, CA. Reprinted by kind permission of the publishers.

E.J. Brill, Leiden. Excerpts from THE NAG HAMMADI LIBRARY ed. James Robertson. Copyright © 1977 E.J. Brill, Leiden, The Netherlands. Reprinted by kind permission of the publishers. Excerpts from THE GOSPEL ACCORDING TO THOMAS, Coptic text established and translated by A. Guillaumont, H.-Ch. Puech, G. Quispel, W. Till and Yassah 'Abd Al Masih. Copyright © 1959 E.J. Brill, Leiden, The Netherlands. Reprinted by kind permission of the publishers.

Burns and Oates Ltd. Excerpt from DARK NIGHT OF THE SOUL by ST. JOHN OF THE CROSS, trans. E. Allison Peers. Copyright © 1976 Search Press Ltd, Burns and Oates Ltd., Tunbridge Wells, Kent. Reprinted by kind permission of the publishers.

Caduceus Magazine, Leamington Spa, UK. Excerpt from article on Alchemy by Llewellyn Vaughan-Lee. Caduceus Magazine issue 19. Reprinted by kind permission of the

Editor of Caduceus and The Golden Sufi Center, Inverness, CA.

Jonathan Cape Ltd. Excerpts from THE HEART OF THE WORLD by Alan Ereira. Jonathan Cape Ltd., London, 1990. Copyright © 1990 Alan Ereira. Reprinted by kind permission of Random House UK Ltd. Excerpts from AN AFRICAN ELEGY by Ben Okri. Jonathan Cape, London 1992. Copyright © Ben Okri 1992. Reprinted by kind permission of Random House UK Ltd.

James Clarke and Co. Ltd. Selected excerpts from THE MYSTICAL THEOLOGY OF THE EASTERN CHURCH by Vladimir Lossky. Copyright 1957 James Clarke and Co. Ltd., Cambridge. Reprinted by kind permission of the publishers.

Anthony Clarke Publishers. Excerpts from SEEDS OF CONTEMPLATION by Thomas Merton. Anthony Clarke Publishers, Wheathamstead, Herts. Copyright © 1961 The Abbey of Gethsemani Inc. Reprinted by kind permission of the publishers.

Columbia University Press. Excerpt from THE PHILOSOPHY OF MARSILIO FICINO by Paul Oskar Kristeller, trans. by Virginia Conant, Columbia University Press, 1943, New York.

Element Books Ltd. Excerpts from THE ROBE OF GLORY by John Davidson. Copyright © John Davidson 1992. Reprinted by kind permission of John Davidson and Element Books Ltd., Shaftesbury, Dorset (Element Inc., Rockport MA, USA). Excerpts from THE GODDESS by Caitlin Matthews. Copyright © 1989 Caitlin Matthews. Reprinted by kind permission of Element Books Ltd., Shaftesbury, Dorset (Element Inc., Rockport MA, USA). Excerpts from MIRROR TO THE LIGHT by Lewis Thompson. Element Books 1984, Shaftesbury, Dorset. Reprinted by kind permission of Richard Lannoy.

Faber and Faber Limited, London. One line from THE COLLECTED POEMS of Wallace Stevens. Reprinted by kind permission of the publishers.

Fount Books, London. Excerpt (Guru Nanak) from UNIVERSAL WISDOM compiled by Bede Griffiths. Copyright © Bede Griffiths 1994.

Garnstone Press. Excerpt from TOUCH THE EARTH, compiled by T.C. McLuhan. Garnstone Press Ltd., 1972. Copyright © 1971 T.C. McLuhan.

George Allen and Unwin Ltd. Excerpts from A TREASURY OF TRADITIONAL WISDOM by Whittall N. Perry. George Allen and Unwin Ltd., London, 1971. Copyright © 1971 George Allen and Unwin.

HarperCollins Publishers Inc. Selected excerpts from ENDURING GRACE: LIVING PORTRAITS OF SEVEN WOMEN MYSTICS by Carol Lee Flinders. Copyright © 1993 by Carol Flinders. Reprinted by permission of HarperCollins Publishers, Inc., New York. Excerpts from WOMEN IN PRAISE OF THE SACRED by Jane Hirshfield. Copyright © 1994 by Jane Hirshfield. Reprinted by permission of Jane Hirshfield and HarperCollins Publishers, Inc., New York. THE TAO THAT CAN BE TOLD...from TAO TE CHING by

Stephen Mitchell. Translation copyright © 1988 by Stephen Mitchell. Reprinted by permission of HarperCollins Publishers, Inc. HOLY SPIRIT... (Hildegarde of Bingen) from THE ENLIGHTENED HEART by Stephen Mitchell. Copyright 1989 by Stephen Mitchell. Reprinted by permission of HarperCollins Publishers, Inc. 9 lines from SOME SAY THAT MY TEACHING IS NONSENSE (Tao Te Ching) from THE ENLIGHTENED HEART by Stephen Mitchell. Reprinted by permission of HarperCollins Publishers,Inc. 3 lines from IN ALL THE TEN DIRECTIONS... (Ryokan) from THE ENLIGHTENED HEART by Stephen Mitchell. Reprinted by permission of HarperCollins Publishers, Inc. Selected excerpts from THE TIBETAN BOOK OF LIVING AND DYING by Sogyal Rinpoche. Copyright © 1993 by Rigpa Fellowship. Reprinted by permission of HarperCollins Publishers, Inc., New York.

HarperCollins Publishers Limited, London. Excerpts from RETURN TO THE CENTRE by Bede Griffiths, Collins Ltd., London 1976. Copyright © 1976 Bede Griffiths. Reprinted by permission of HarperCollins Publishers Limited, London.

Holland Library, Washington State University. Three excerpts from the unpublished poems of Lewis Thompson. Reprinted by kind permission of John Guido, Head, Manuscripts Archives and Special Collections.

Alfred A. Knopf Inc., New York. One line from THE COLLECTED POEMS of Wallace Stevens, reprinted by kind permission of the publishers.

Longman's Green. Excerpts from THE REVELATIONS OF MECHTHILD OF MAGDEBURG or THE FLOWING LIGHT OF THE GODHEAD by Lucy Menzies. Longman's Green, London 1953. Copyright © The Iona Community, Glasgow. Reprinted by kind permission of the Iona Community.

Meerama Publications. Excerpts from LOVE'S FIRE by Andrew Harvey. Meerama Publications, Ithaca, NY. Copyright © 1988 Andrew Harvey. Reprinted by kind permission of the publisher.

Quest Books. Excerpts from MOTHER OF THE UNIVERSE by Lex Hixon. Quest Books, Wheaton, Ill. Copyright 1994 Lex Hixon. Reprinted by kind permission of the author.

Macmillan & Co. Excerpts from ONE HUNDRED POEMS OF KABIR, trans. by Rabindranath Tagore assisted by Evelyn Underhill. Macmillan & Co. London, 1961. Reprinted by kind permission of the publishers.

New Directions Publishing Corp. Excerpts from NEW SEEDS OF CONTEMPLATION by Thomas Merton. Copyright © 1961 The Abbey of Gethsemani Inc. Reprinted by kind permission of New Directions Publishing Corp., New York. Excerpts from THE WISDOM OF THE DESERT by Thomas Merton. Copyright © 1960 The Abbey of Gethsemani, Inc. Reprinted by kind permission of New Directions Publishing Corp., New York. Excerpts from THE

POEMS OF ST. JOHN OF THE CROSS, trans. by Willis Barnstone. Copyright © 1972 Willis Barstone. Reprinted by kind permission of New Directions Publishing Corp., New York.

Oxford University Press. Excerpts from A SLEEP OF PRISONERS by Christopher Fry. Oxford University Press, 1985. Reprinted by kind permission of Oxford University Press.

Penguin Books Ltd. Excerpts from THE UPANISHADS trans. Juan Mascaro. Penguin Classics 1965, London. Copyright © 1965 Juan Mascaro. Reprinted by permission of Penguin Books Ltd. Excerpts from THE BHAGAVAD GITA trans. JUAN MASCARO. Penguin Classics 1962, London. Copyright © 1962 Juan Mascaro. Reprinted by permission of Penguin Books Ltd. 5 lines from p. 159 and 12 lines from p. 100 from MILLENIUM by David Maybury-Lewis (Viking 1992). Copyright © 1992 Meech Grant Productions Ltd, David Maybury-Lewis and The Body Shop International plc, 1992. Reproduced by permission of Penguin Books Ltd. *The Song of the Man Who Has Come Through*, by D.H. Lawrence, reprinted from THE COMPLETE POEMS OF D.H. LAWRENCE, collected and edited by Vivian de Sola Pinto and F. Warren Roberts. Copyright © 1964, 1971 by Angelo Ravagli and C.M. Weekley, Executors of the Estate of Frieda Lawrence Ravagli. All rights reserved. Reprinted by permission of Viking Penguin, a division of Penguin Books, USA, Inc., and the Estate of Frieda Lawrence Ravagli.

Penguin Books Canada Limited. The Selection from MILLENIUM. Copyright © Meech Grant Productions Ltd, David Maybury-Lewis and The Body Shop International plc, 1992. Reprinted by kind permission of Penguin Books Canada Limited.

Routledge and Kegan Paul Ltd. Excerpt from THE SECRET OF THE GOLDEN FLOWER trans. and explained by Richard Wilhelm, with a commentary by C.G. Jung. English trans. Cary F. Baynes. Routledge and Kegan Paul Ltd. 1931, 1957. Reprinted by kind permission of Routledge and Kegan Paul Ltd. and Harcourt, Brace, Jovanovich Inc., Orlando, Florida.

Routledge and Kegan Paul, New York. Excerpt from THE CRYSTAL AND THE WAY OF LIGHT: SUTRA, TANTRA AND DZOGCHEN. Compiled and edited by John Shane. Routledge and Kegan Paul, New York, 1987. Reprinted by kind permission of the publishers.

Schocken Books Inc. Excerpts from TALES OF THE HASIDIM by Martin Buber. Schocken Books Inc., New York. Copyright Schocken Books Inc., 1947, 1975. Reprinted by kind permission of the publishers.

Sierra Club Books. Excerpts from THE DREAM OF THE EARTH by Thomas Berry. Sierra Club Books, San Francisco CA. Copyright © 1988 Thomas Berry. Reprinted by kind permission of the publishers. Shambhala Publications Inc. Excerpt from GREAT SWAN; MEETINGS WITH RAMAKRISHNA by Lex Hixon. Shambhala, Boston and London. Copyright ©

1992 Lex Hixon. Reprinted by kind permission of the author. Excerpt from AWAKENING TO THE TAO by Liu I-Ming trans. from the Chinese by Thomas Cleary. Shambhala Publications Inc., Boston MA 1988. Copyright © 1988 Thomas Cleary. Reprinted by kind permission of Shambhala Publications Inc. Excerpts from LEAVING MY FATHER'S HOUSE by Marion Woodman. Shambhala Publications Inc., Boston MA., 1992. Copyright © 1992 Marion Woodman. Reprinted by kind permission of Shambhala Publications Inc. Excerpts from THE BOOK OF THE HEART by Loy Ching-Yuen. Shambhala Publications Inc. 1994. Reprinted by kind permission of Shambhala Publications Inc. Excerpt from VITALITY, ENERGY, SPIRIT (Liu I-Ming) trans. and edited by Thomas Cleary. Copyright © by Thomas Cleary 1991. Reprinted by kind permission of Shambhala Publications Inc., Boston, MA.

Soncino Press. Excerpts from THE ZOHAR, 1-5, trans. Harry Sperling and Maurice Simon. Soncino Press, 1931-4.

Sri Aurobindo Ashram Trust. Excerpts from THE LIFE DIVINE and SAVITRI by Sri Aurobindo. Copyright © Sri Aurobindo Ashram Trust 1939, 1990, Pondicherry, India. Reprinted by kind permission of the Ashram Trust.

State University of New York Press. Excerpt from THE SUFI PATH OF LOVE by William Chittick. Copyright © 1984 William Chittick. Reprinted by kind permission of State University of New York Press.

The excerpts from WANG WEI, CHI HSI, an anonymous Taoist sage and YU SHI-NAN (treatise on the Marrow of the Brush) are from CREATIVITY AND TAOISM by CHANG CHUNG-YUAN, Wildwood House, London, 1963. Copyright © 1963 Chang Chung-Yuan.

The excerpt DAILY WORD is taken from p. 135 of THE BOOK OF RUNES with a commentary by Ralph Blum. Oracle Books, Los Angeles, 1982; Headline Book Publishing plc, London 1993. Copyright © Ralph Blum. The excerpts from Meister Eckhart are from MEISTER ECKHART, A MODERN TRANSLATION trans. Raymond B. Blakney, New York, 1941; MEISTER ECKHART, WORKS, trans. by C. de B. Evans, London, 1924 and MEISTER ECKHART, vol. 1, trans. by C. de B. Evans 1956; MEISTER ECKHART, SERMONS AND TREATISES, VOL. 1 trans. M. O'C Walsh, London 1979.

The excerpts from Julian of Norwich are from JULIAN OF NORWICH: REVELATIONS OF DIVINE LOVE, trans. and with an introduction by Clifton Wolters, Penguin Books, London 1966; JULIAN OF NORWICH: SHOWINGS, trans. and with an introduction by Edmund Colledge, O.S. A. and James Walsh, S.J., Paulist Press, New York, 1978.

The excerpts from Jan of Ruysbroeck are from THE ADORNMENT OF THE SPIRITUAL MARRIAGE, THE BOOK OF TRUTH, THE SPARKLING STONE trans. by C.A. Wynschenk Dom, Dutton & Co, New York, and J.M. Dent & Sons Ltd., London, 1916.

The excerpts from the Tao Teh King are taken from the THE WAY AND ITS POWER by Arthur Waley, George Allen and Unwin Ltd., 1934, the translation by Gia-Fu Feng and Jane English, Wildwood House, London 1973 and translations by Stephen Mitchell in THE ENLIGHTENED HEART, Harper & Row, New York, 1989 (see above under HarperCollins).

The excerpts from St. Peter of Alcantara and Maragall are taken from the introduction to THE UPANISHADS by Juan Mascaro, Penguin Classics, London, 1962.

The excerpts from St. Teresa of Avila are from THE INTERIOR CASTLE, trans. by E. Allison Peers; TERESA OF AVILA, THE COLLECTED WORKS, 3 vols. trans. by Kieran Kavanaugh, O.C.D., and Otilio Rodriguez, O.C.D., Institute of Carmelite Studies, Washington D.C. 1980, and THE WAY OF PERFECTION trans. Alice Alexander, The Mercier Press, Cork.

We would like to express our thanks to Elizabeth Collins and to the editor of The Golgonooza Press for permission to quote from the writings of the artist Cecil Collins in THE VISION OF THE FOOL, Golgonooza Press, London, 1994. Also to Richard Lannoy for permission to quote excerpts from MIRROR TO THE LIGHT by Lewis Thompson; to Jane Hirshfield for permission to reproduce her translations of Mechthild of Magdeburg in WOMEN IN PRAISE OF THE SACRED; and to China Galland for permission to use the Dzogchen excerpt on p.345 of LONGING FOR DARKNESS.

Grateful acknowledgement is made to the Tate Gallery, London for permission to reproduce Cecil Collins' The Angel of the Flowing Light and to the National Gallery, London, for permission to reproduce St. Jerome in a Mountainous Landscape, attributed to Joachim Patenier and to Robin Baring for illustrations on pp. 39 and 174.

The Publishers would like to thank the following sources for permission to reproduce their visual material. Every effort has been made to contact copyright holders and the Publishers would like to apologise for any inadvertent errors and will be pleased to correct these in subsequent editions.

Ancient Art and Architecture Collection, Anne Baring, Robin Baring, Jean Dieuzaide, C. M. Dixon – Photo resources The National Gallery, San Marco Museum, The Tate Gallery, Werner Forman Archive Ltd